The Q Guide to

Wonder Woman

The Q Guides

FROM ALYSON BOOKS

AVAILABLE NOW:

POP CULTURE

Q GUIDE

OUT THERE

The Q Guide to

Wonder Woman

Stuff You Didn't Even Know You Wanted to Know . . . about Lynda Carter, the iconic TV show, and one amazing costume

[**Mike Pingel**]

alyson books
NEW YORK

*I dedicate this book to Scott Jonson, Brian Lamberson,
and Joey Marshall. All three of you are my
"superheroes" because all of you make my artistic
endeavors worthwhile and painless.
(And boy can I be a pain!)
Thank you, Wonder Angels!*

© 2008 BY MIKE PINGEL
ALL RIGHTS RESERVED

MANUFACTURED IN THE UNITED STATES OF AMERICA

PUBLISHED BY ALYSON BOOKS
245 WEST 17TH STREET,
NEW YORK, NY 10011

DISTRIBUTION IN THE UNITED KINGDOM BY
TURNAROUND PUBLISHER SERVICES LTD.
UNIT 3, OLYMPIA TRADING ESTATE
COBURG ROAD, WOOD GREEN
LONDON N22 6TZ ENGLAND

FIRST EDITION: OCTOBER 2008

08 09 10 11 12 13 14 15 16 17 **a** 10 9 8 7 6 5 4 3 2 1

ISBN: 1-59350-080-7
ISBN-13: 978-1-59350-080-1

LIBRARY OF CONGRESS CATALOGING-IN-PUBLICATION DATA
ARE ON FILE.

COVER DESIGN BY VICTOR MINGOVITS

Contents

Contents

Introduction

WHENEVER I think of Wonder Woman, I always think of Lynda Carter. In 1975, she took on the role and literally became America's Wonder Woman. Carter empowered women with her portrayal of the comic book character and became one of the world's celebrated superhero icons.

I had the pleasure of meeting Lynda Carter in San Francisco when she was performing her cabaret show. She was as mesmerizing and warm as one would expect. Today and forever, she will be our Wonder Woman.

I hope this Q Guide to TV's Wonder Woman brings back a lot of fun memories of Lynda Carter and the series. And remember that, whether you spin to the left or to the right, Wonder Woman is only a flash of light away! . . . and I'm spinning right now!

—*Mike Pingel*

The Q Guide to
Wonder Woman

Lynda Carter and Mike Pingel backstage after her 2007
cabaret show in San Francisco. (© Mike Pingel)

CHAPTER ONE

The Wondrous Story

IN 1941, psychologist William Moulton Marston, who created the polygraph, was hired to be an educational consultant for All-American Publications and National Periodicals, which would later merge and become DC Comics. In the already male-dominated superhero comic world, Marston came up with the idea for the first female superhero, Wonder Woman. He created a background for her that was steeped in Greek mythology and was the source of her power.

In the world of comics, Wonder Woman was introduced as a part of the "Justice League," in which she fought crime side by side with her male counterparts: Superman, Batman, the Flash, Green Lantern, Aquaman, and the Martian Manhunter.

In the early sixties, producer Douglas S. Cramer thought a comic strip should be put on television two or three times a week. He had originally worked with Procter & Gamble on daytime serials and was really enthusiastic about bringing the daytime serial formula to nighttime, which he similarly did with *Peyton Place* (1964) on ABC.

With the success of *Peyton Place* three nights a week, Cramer sold the network on his comic strip idea. They immediately went out to secure the rights to produce Dick Tracy and were unsuccessful.

Cramer had been a huge Batman fan growing up. Every Halloween as a kid he wore the Batman outfit, with one of his friends as Robin. So when he brought them the idea of doing Batman, ABC-TV thought he was kind of crazy and he was asked if he could get anybody in Hollywood to take him seriously.

"There was a wonderful man named Bill Dozier who had run RKO and then Screen Gems, who was now an independent producer. I went to him with the (Batman) idea and he got on it immediately. I had secured the rights at ABC. Twentieth Century Fox put up the money and Batman was launched and on the air," Cramer remembers. "The first test screening of *Batman* went very badly, but the show was already set to go on the air in five days. The production added all the animation and the bat wipes (POW, WHACK) and changed the score, so the audience didn't take a moment of it seriously and it became a giant hit."

"It's interesting that both *Batman* and *Charlie's Angels* received low test scores from a preview audience. No one would admit they actually liked the shows, or there was something fundamentally wrong with the concept, and they didn't respond to it in a closed screening."

"The Adam West version of *Batman* ran twice a week for four years. There was always a cliffhanger which started one night and finished the next. We tried this concept again with the *Green Hornet* starring a young oriental performer that the network didn't think would become a star, named Bruce Lee. The show flopped and it was off the air in thirteen weeks. But Bruce went on to stardom."

PARADISE TIPS

Her sister, Wonder Girl, was already on television, seen in the 1967 animated series the *Superman/Aquaman Hour* in the "Teen Titans" segments.

While producing *Batman*, Bill Dozier decided to create a four-and-a-half-minute screen test: "Wonder Woman: Who's Afraid of Diana Prince?" It starred Ellie Wood Walker as Wonder Woman, Maudie Prickett as her mother, and Linda Harrison as Diana's Wonder Woman alter ego. The test was produced by Greenway Productions.

The short pilot centers around the homebody Diana Prince/Wonder Woman who lives at home with her mother. As Diana Prince goes behind a turning bookcase she would emerge as the beautiful, sexy Wonder Woman. The show was not picked up by ABC-TV since it was too similar to *Batgirl,* which was already in development. Also, the network had had two other superhero shows, *Captain Nice* and *Mr. Terrific,* fail.

As much as they tried, TV was not able to hold Wonder Woman back; she emerged on December 2, 1972, in the animated cartoon *The Brady Kids* in the episode "It's All Greek to Me." The Brady kids are transported back to ancient Greece and meet Wonder Woman. While there, they compete in an Olympic marathon and win. However, Wonder Woman suggests they give up the title because it would change history.

Lynda Carter, Miss Arizona, won the title of Miss World USA in 1972.

Wonder Woman was quickly picked up in 1973 as a part of the new animated series *Super Friends,* which ran for sixteen episodes. She was voiced by actress Shannon Farnon who later voiced Wonder Woman in the 1978 animated series *Challenge of the Super Friends,* which also had sixteen episodes.

In 1974, Warner Brothers produced the first official pilot of *Wonder Woman.* Cathy Lee Crosby, former professional tennis player turned actress, was given the lead role. In this incarnation, Wonder Woman was given an updated seventies look. She had blonde hair and traded her tiara, bracelets, and lasso in for a red, white, and blue tennis-style outfit. Although the show was slightly

Cathy Lee Crosby played Wimbledon twice and ranked #7 in singles and #4 in doubles in the United States. Crosby went on to star in the NBC hit *That's Incredible,* wrote the best-selling self-help book *Let the Magic Begin,* and continues to produce projects with her own company.

off the mark, it brought in very strong ratings. "I had nothing to do with it," remarks Cramer. "It lacked style and distinction and tested badly, but when it went on the air as a movie of the week it got great numbers."

After receiving solid ratings with the *Wonder Woman* pilot, Warner Brothers decided it was time to take another try at it, with a new Wonder Woman and a new producer to guide it. Cramer was selected to take over. He understood the woman's movement and felt that Wonder Woman would be a great beacon for women's lib. "We did a new pilot and went back to the original comic book, which they hadn't done with the Cathy Lee Crosby [pilot]. We started back in the days of Greek heroines and mythology and showed where Wonder Woman came from, and then brought her to World War II, thinking that you needed heroes and some identifiable heavies that had the same kind of mythology attached to them that Wonder Woman did to make it all acceptable to an seventies audience."

Writer Stanley Ralph Ross had a big hand in the history of Wonder Woman coming to TV. Back in the sixties, he was writing for the superhero hit TV show *Batman*. "Stanley Ralph Ross wrote the original *Wonder Woman* pilot for me. He had done some of the most

PARADISE TIPS

Lynda Carter had auditioned for the 1974 *Wonder Woman* pilot, but lost the part to Cathy Lee Crosby.

PARADISE TIPS

After writing the pilot for *Batman*, Lorenzo Semple went on to write for feature films including *Three Days of the Condor, King Kong, Sheena,* and 007's *Never Say Never Again.*

successful *Batman* episodes, so I purposely went back to get him to do it. I actually tried to get the man who wrote the *Batman* pilot, a very noted screenwriter by the name of Lorenzo Semple Jr., and he wouldn't do it. He just thought he was too big for television then."

The New Original Wonder Woman pilot script was created with Wonder Woman and her alter ego Diana Prince coming to the aid of the United States as the assistant to war hero Major Steve Trevor during World War II. The creative team had decided to keep it true to the original comic book, which included a comic strip-style opening sequence and comic bubbles throughout the episode.

With a script written, the search was on in Hollywood to find a tall, busty actress with an angelic face to

PARADISE TIPS

Lynda Carter had $25 in the bank the day she received the call informing her that she won the coveted role of Wonder Woman.

be Wonder Woman. This was not an easy task. "Alan Shayne, who was the head of casting at Warner Brothers, found Lynda Carter and brought her to me. I loved her. We went into the network and sold her," remembers Cramer.

The producers had seen Carter in a previous screen test for *The Fan*. She was told she would not have to audition for the role of Wonder Woman, but would have to film a couple of screen tests, one as Diana Prince, which she tested with soon-to-be costar Lyle Waggoner, and the second as an athletic endurance as Wonder Woman in a thrown-together outfit.

Many of the brass at ABC-TV and Warner Brothers were concerned that Carter was too green to be carrying her own TV series. Cramer had a gut feeling that Carter was right and kept pushing for her. Finally he was given the green light for his choice.

The casting of her costar was a little easier. While rewriting the pilot, writer Stanley Ralph Ross had run into Lyle Waggoner on the Warner Brothers lot. Waggoner asked if Ross was working on anything and to

PARADISE TIPS

Lyle Waggoner worked as the straight man on *The Carol Burnett Show* and was the first nude (with no frontal nudity) centerfold for *Playgirl* magazine in June 1973. As the series progressed, he was also elected mayor of Encino, California, in 1976.

PARADISE TIPS

In scenes with Lynda Carter, Cloris Leachman would stand on a platform so she would appear to be the same height as Carter.

think of him. Ross felt that Waggoner would be a perfect fit to play Major Steve Trevor and wrote the role with him in mind. During the auditions for Steve Trevor, the production had looked at a host of candidates, but as soon as Waggoner auditioned, he was Cramer and Warner's only choice and was given the role.

Other pilot casting included John Randolph as General Blankenship, Golden Globe winner Stella Stevens as Marcia (and evil Nazi Agent M.), Oscar winner Cloris Leachman as Queen Hippolyta, and Fannie Flagg as the Amazon Doctor. With the main characters cast, the newest revival pilot of *Wonder Woman* began shooting in late 1975.

PARADISE TIPS

Fannie Flagg in real life is an open lesbian who went on to be an Oscar nominee for writing *Fried Green Tomatoes* in 1991, and she also wrote for Dolly Parton's TV Show *Dolly* in 1987. Flagg continued to work as an actor in the film *Grease* and as a series regular in *Harper Valley P.T.A.*

The Pilot: Red, White, and Blue

Oscar-nominated designer Donfeld went to work to create the patriotic Wonder Woman outfit. The first day Carter arrived on set and put on the outfit, she was greeted with a thunderous applause from the cast and crew; however, the costume was a little uncomfortable for Carter. The golden-breasted top was bowed like a corset in the front to keep the outfit from falling down and made it impossible for Carter to sit down. Between takes Carter would lean against a slant board in order to rest. The idea came from a crew member who had seen Elizabeth Taylor use one while filming another movie.

The pilot showcased some pretty fantastic special effects never before seen on TV. Wonder Woman's bracelets were supposed to deflect bullets. The bracelets were

PARADISE TIPS

Wonder Woman's outfit originally had a removable skirt that went over her shorts in the pilot episode. Throughout the first season, she rarely wore the skirt at the request of the network. The skirt makes its final appearance in the episode "Last of the Two-Dollar Bills" (episode 9) and never appeared during the CBS years.

PARADISE TIPS

The opening scenes of Paradise Island were filmed on location in Malibu, California.

wired with small explosives and Carter would hold a small firing mechanism in her hand and would push a button to ignite the charge.

Wonder Woman's invisible plane shows just how smart and crafty the special effects people were on the show. A life-size Plexiglas plane was constructed and filmed against a blue screen to create the realism of the invisible plane.

With the series set in the 1940s, much attention was focused on the sets to keep the feel of that decade, which included the cars, buildings, streets, clothes, and hairstyles. Many of the dresses came directly from the Warner Brothers wardrobe archives. Some of Stella Stevens's costumes were originally worn by Joan Crawford, Barbara Stanwyck, and Virginia Mayo.

PARADISE TIPS

A special trick was used in order for Wonder Woman to carry Steve Trevor to the hospital. They had Lyle Waggoner lying on a 2 x 4 wooden board with guys on each side of him crawling on the floor holding the board up.

DONFELD: TWIRLING COSTUMES

Donfeld was the man behind the Wonder Woman. Donfeld was a much sought-after costume designer in Hollywood, having been Academy Award–nominated for Costume Design four times, for the films *Days of Wine and Roses; They Shoot Horses, Don't They?; Tom Sawyer;* and *Prizzi's Honor.*

His full name was Donald Lee Feld and he later shortened it to Donfeld after his name was often misspelled. He began his career in Hollywood in 1953 as an art designer for Capital Records, where he created album covers. He went on to design costumes for the Academy Awards musical numbers. He worked on over fifty films as costume designer. His work was beloved by many actresses; he did exclusive work for Jill St. John in *Diamonds are Forever* and for Jacqueline Bisset in the TV film *Choices.* He returned to his sci-fi roots on Mel Brooks's *Spaceballs.*

When he was brought on to the *Wonder Woman* set he was asked to design the 1975 *Wonder Woman* outfit. His sketches brought the producers excitement, yet they were unsure if they had the money to do the outfit. Donfeld pulled the 1975 outfit together for the first season, but when the second season rolled around the production had all the money to create his complete all-American Wonder Woman outfit to save the world on a weekly basis.

All of Wonder Woman's accessories where made for the TV version. Her bracelets were created to hold small explosives to create the look of Wonder Woman deflecting bullets. Her tiara was made out of gold bouillon leather, which is used to make shoes, and her motorcycle helmet was also custom made.

Donfeld had fun creating several secondary outfits for Wonder Woman from the motorcycle outfit, which was a body suit. He also created a never seen two-piece red, white, and blue bathing suit that would be Wonder Woman's aqua outfit, but the suit would not fit Lynda Carter so the production decided to use the motorcycle suit as a substitute.

Donfeld's charm and style as a designer brought so much to the series. He was a maverick of his talent, creating outfits separate from the comic books and establishing the series' own identity that still is strong today.

In 1978, Donfeld received the only Emmy Award nomination for the series *Wonder Woman,* for Outstanding Achievement in Costume Design for a Drama or Comedy Series for the episode "Anschluss '77".

Donfeld passed away in 2007 in Los Angeles from natural causes. Donfeld's outfits for the show have become as iconic as Wonder Woman herself.

Emmy Award–winner Charles Fox composed the music that set the tone of the movie. It bridged the scenes to let the audience know what was happening.

One of the main hurdles to overcome was Diana's transition into Wonder Woman. Carter had suggested to the director that she could do a spin. Diana Prince

PARADISE TIPS

For the filming of the pilot, Lynda Carter's hair was styled for Wonder Woman. The styling was so harsh on her hair that when the show went to series Carter wore a wig instead.

started the spin and transformed into Wonder Woman holding Diana's clothing. Carter showed her spin idea to Cramer, who thought it was great, and the spin was incorporated exclusively into the TV series.

Another obstacle to overcome was Carter's eyesight. Having poor eyesight, Carter would have to count out her movements while filming scenes and even use the warmth of the lights to hit her camera marks. The production crew would use sand bags to let her know where she would have to stop if they were critical shots.

PARADISE TIPS

Diana turning into Wonder Woman was the biggest expense in the pilot due to the stop-action camera special effects.

"Wonder Woman got on the air because of a young guy at ABC-TV who believed in it, by the name of Brandon Tartikoff. Tartikoff fought for the show and it was successful, but it was never a runaway hit. After he left ABC-TV, the network tried to make the story more realistic and believable."

—Douglas S. Cramer

The pilot film aired on ABC-TV on November 7, 1975, to very solid ratings. Since ABC hadn't signed the show on as a series, a bidding war began between the TV networks. ABC eventually bought two more episodes that aired as specials in April 1976: "Wonder Woman Meets Baroness Von Gunther" and "Fausta, the Nazi Wonder Woman." Both brought in great numbers. ABC still had not placed the show on their fall lineup. NBC was prepared to buy the series if ABC decided to pass on it for that season. This forced ABC to continue their partnership with Wonder Woman. On July 12, 1976, ABC announced that they were proud to add *The New Original Wonder Woman* to their fall lineup.

The ABCs of Season One

As the first season was officially in production, there were many well-known guest stars hired to appear on the show, including Dick Van Patten, John Saxon, Carolyn Jones, Robert Reed, Tim O'Connor, and Roy Rogers.

One major change was the elimination of the slow motion striptease used in the pilot and the two specials. They were too costly to do in the series. A flash of light during the spin was added to make the transformation faster. It became a trademark of the series.

Lynda Carter at first enjoyed doing many of her own stunts; however, the studio frowned on it because they feared that she would hurt herself, which would cause a delay in the production. Luckily, she never injured herself.

The network execs, the producers, and the majority of the production crew were men. They had many conversations about some of Wonder Woman's lines going too far promoting feminism. They didn't take into consideration that there was a strong group of women writers who wrote many of the scripts.

Throughout this season, the chemistry between the two lead characters was very strong. There were fears that if their relationship developed into something more serious, they would eventually marry. This would become the downfall of the series, so their sizzling romance

ANDY MANGELS ON DONFELD AND THE COSTUMES

Best-selling author and DVD producer Andy Mangels is also the author of *The Wonder Woman Companion* (2009) and a diehard Wonder Woman fan. He interviewed almost everyone related to the TV series, and had the pleasure of chatting with the late costume designer Donfeld, who passed away in 2007.

To clothe a custom-built, life-sized Lynda Carter mannequin in his office, Mangels and his partner recreated Donfeld's Wonder Woman costume from a pattern taken from an original costume that Lynda Carter had worn. Using a clear shower curtain and a Sharpie pen, he traced the costume all the way down to the tiny beads of the golden eagle on the corset, and to the position of the stars on the shorts. Mangels shares some of Donfeld's designing insights:

"Donfeld was credited with the design of the original TV's Wonder Woman outfits. If you look at the World War II–era costumes used for ABC, they were essentially the same as what was in the comic book. However, he modified how the eagle wings went together, and completely designed the cape.

"Most people didn't realize that the stars on the cape

were only on one side. It was perceived that they were on both due to the cape being flipped around during the photo sessions Lynda did with it. The initial concept was to have the stars on the outside, and have the inside look like an American flag.

"On the costume used for CBS, it was Donfeld's re-design. It was a departure from what had been done before, adding the spread-eagle wings, the V shape on the stars on the shorts and their new 'French cut,' and changing the bracelets to gold.

"Donfeld also designed the Wonder Wet Suit. It was created after he tried to make a Wonder Bikini. The Wonder Bikini didn't quite fit Lynda, so they decided to go with a Wonder Wet Suit instead. Then they added a gold helmet and used it as the Wonder Biker outfit. For the Wonder Skateboard outfit, they added a red helmet to her regular costume along with elbow and knee pads to show kids that they need to be safe. The message was, if Wonder Woman needs to be safe, then you need to be safe too.

"Everyone on the series was clear on the fact that they wanted a sexy superhero. An interesting element is that Lynda is wearing more clothing than the bikini-clad Charlie's Angels wore on the beach. Who dressed sexier, Wonder Woman or Charlie's Angels? Most people would say Wonder Woman, because she always wore an exposed top and had her legs exposed. However, if you look closely at her outfit, it covers everything."

was put on the back burner to cool. It became nonexistent in the following seasons. In the comic books, Steve Trevor and Wonder Woman eventually did marry and had a daughter named Lyta (named after Wonder Woman's mother, Queen Hippolyta) who became superhero Fury.

Even though the show had decent ratings, ABC decided not to renew the series for a second season. Since NBC and CBS had originally fought for the series, would they be interested in it now? Not even a golden lasso could answer this question.

PARADISE TIPS

Lynda Carter was to portray the Playboy Playmate in the 1979 Francis Ford Coppola film, *Apocalypse Now*.

CBS Lassos Wonder Woman

"After ABC canceled *Wonder Woman*, CBS picked it up on the condition that it would be made contemporary," remembers Cramer, "so we produced another two years where we brought in Bruce Lansbury, who had produced many *Mission: Impossible* episodes when I was running Paramount, and he was considered a more realistic game player."

With the modern-day element brought into the series, the opening theme was rewritten, Carter's wardrobe became high fashion, and the storylines began to resemble other shows like *Charlie's Angels* and *Bionic Woman*. Another major change was Wonder Woman's outfit. It went from a conservative 1940s look to a more defined style by giving her a flashier bustier, shorts with a higher leg, and bracelets that were matched to her golden lasso and tiara. She was also given a set of new outfits to wear for underwater, motorcycling, and skateboarding scenes.

PARADISE TIPS

Donfeld originally designed a red, white, and blue two-piece bikini for Lynda to wear, but due to her increasing weight loss it had to be resized several times. Because of this, a full-body wet suit was used instead.

PARADISE TIPS

Lynda Carter was really a Wonder Woman herself! One evening while filming a stunt, Carter decided to do it herself. She ran and grabbed the strut of the helicopter and told them to fly up about thirty feet. They got the shot and returned her to the ground. The next day, Carter was reprimanded by the studio for putting herself in danger.

Another change was Lyle Waggoner's role from Major Steve Trevor to playing his look-alike son, Steve Trevor Jr., a field agent for the Inter-Agency Defense Command (IADC), and Diana Prince becoming his field partner. Also working for the IADC were new cast members Normann Burton as Joe Atkinson and Sandra Sharp as Eve. They received their assignments from their unseen boss. As the season progressed, the unseen boss was written out, and Steve began to hand out the assignments. The IRAC computer (aka IRA) was introduced and began to help out with vital information. Rover, a roving computer, was introduced in "IRAC Is Missing" (episode 31).

PARADISE TIPS

In 1978, Lynda Carter was crowned "The Most Beautiful Woman in the World" by the International Academy of Beauty and the British Press Organization.

After nine episodes, the Joe Atkinson character was let go. His responsibilities were given to Steve Trevor Jr., as Diana took the complete lead in all the investigations.

The Final Wonder

The third season went through a few more changes. The opening sequence was revamped with a new synthesized disco theme. Eve was gone. Steve Trevor Jr. was reduced to brief appearances and was eventually written out of the series. With fewer characters around, Rover's role became larger as the show's joke-telling sidekick. Rover did speak a bit, but mainly used "the Roadrunner" sounds.

As the new season began, *Wonder Woman* was beating out the competition in the ratings; however, in November 1979, NBC debuted the new sitcom *Diff'rent Strokes,* which became a huge success and took away

PARADISE TIPS

A proposed spin-off from the episode "The Man Who Could Not Die" was set to star Olympic gold medalist Bob Seagren as an indestructible superhero. Similar spin-offs for Debra Winger as Wonder Girl and Julie Anne Haddock as the super-powered girl in the episode "The Girl from Ilandia" were also being considered. Unfortunately, none of the potential series was ever picked up.

THE WONDROUS POWERS OF HER OUTFIT

The golden belt is a symbol of Amazon woman-
hood and it keeps her strength intact when she
is off Paradise Island.

The golden lasso is made out of an indestructible
material. When it is draped around anyone it
has the power to compel that person to tell
the truth and to erase memories.

The bracelets are made out of feminum metal,
found only on Paradise Island, and are used to
deflect bullets.

The golden tiara can be used as a communica-
tion device to keep in contact with Paradise
Island and, when needed, can be used as a
boomerang.

many of *Wonder Woman*'s younger viewers. To help
improve the ratings, Diana Prince moved to Los Angeles, Steve Trevor Jr. was gone, and they brought in teenage idol Clark Brandon.

As the season came to a close, CBS decided not to
bring the series back. The network's final statement was
that the show was "temporarily shelved." The final episode aired on September 11, 1979. After sixty episodes,

PARADISE TIPS

two networks, and endless spins, TV's Wonder Woman took her final bow.

Wonder Film Rumor

Producers Leonard Goldberg (creator/producer of *Charlie's Angels*) and Joel Silver (producer of "Matrix," "Die Hard," and "Lethal Weapon" films) are set to produce the Wonder Woman feature film. Due to rumored script issues the film has not gone any further, yet Sandra Bullock, Katie Holmes, Lucy Lawless, and Catherine Zeta-Jones all have been candidates for the role of Wonder Woman for the feature.

In 2006, Joss Whedon, who created and produced *Buffy, The Vampire Slayer*, was on board to write and direct the Wonder Woman flick. New casting rumors included Sarah Michelle Gellar, Charisma Carpenter, Jessica Alba, Mischa Barton, Lindsay Lohan, Nadia Bjorlin, and Kate Beckinsale for the lead.

YouTube.com has also brought a new breath to the search for the new Wonder Woman, with actresses

During the November 8, 1999, online chat for Lens Express, Lynda Carter weighed in with her ideas about who should take over the feature role of Wonder Woman: either Catherine Zeta-Jones or Cindy Crawford.

such as Blythe Metz submitting their tapes to the film's producers, Leonard Goldberg and Joel Silver, via the Web site.

Most recently, Warner Brothers was getting ready to shoot the feature film *Justice League of America* with the role of Wonder Woman rumored to be played by Australian model Megan Gale. The film was written by Kieran Mulroney and Michelle Mulroney and was to be directed by Oscar winner George Miller. Unfortunately, the film was shelved just prior to shooting.

Rumors still float around Hollywood about the feature. Most recently, it was posted that Morena Baccarin

PARADISE TIPS

Lynda Carter still has one of the original costumes she wore as Wonder Woman on the series. She has only brought it out for show-and-tell for her kids during elementary school.

was rumored take the lead and Anne Hathaway will take over the role.

The saddest news in the journey of having a Wonder Woman feature film come to reality was that *Buffy* creator Joss Whedon left the director's seat of the film due to "creative differences."

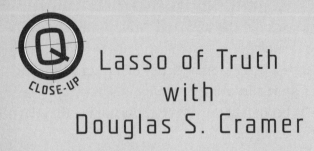

Lasso of Truth
with
Douglas S. Cramer

"Wonder Woman" *was about the time I came out of the closet with a vengeance."*

—Douglas S. Cramer

Did you like it when they brought the series into modern times?
I didn't like it and I tried to convince them otherwise. CBS thought strongly enough about it and made it a condition for getting picked up. So rather than see the show canceled, Warner's TV president Alan Shayne decided we had to try it.

For me personally, the last two years of the show lacked the spark and the fun that it was in the beginning—we became kind of a retooled version of *The Bionic Woman,* with a better costume.

I must say in retrospect, I think they finally got it right with *Batman,* after twenty-five years of tinkering with its features. They lost their focus and started questioning what they were doing after a couple of films. They made some bad Batman movies and now they are brilliantly back on track with the new Christian Bale versions. Those were all the things that poor Wonder Woman went through and never got back to basics, which maybe a film of Wonder Woman would do.

Why did you choose Lyle Waggoner?
Lyle was a sketch comic from *Carol Burnett* and seemed squared-jawed perfect, like a living Ken doll. He was infinitely more successful in the first two seasons. The last year he was written around and was not a vital character. In some ways Lynda had an easier time playing the last two years. By then she had learned a lot more about acting and could play the contemporary Wonder Woman fairly straight forward.

Who else was up for the role of Wonder Woman?
There were dozens of people that were considered by the network, the studio, and me. I know there was some serious thought given to Jill St. John. Also Stella Stevens's, Angie Dickenson's, and Barbara Eden's names came up. The real hope always was discovering somebody new. That was one of the problems with Cathy Lee Crosby—she was selected more for TV fan appeal than being right for the role. Lindsay Wagner was so successful as the Bionic Woman partially because she came out of nowhere and created her own image.

What was your gut reaction when you first saw Lynda Carter?
She was Wonder Woman. She had great charm, was incredibly beautiful, and had a fantastic body. You believed her. She is extraordinarily sincere and like a great big Girl Scout just facing the world. I think that paid off for the character. Lynda has remained a dear friend.

I understand you had to fight ABC to keep Lynda.
It was not easy. They felt she did not have enough experience and they were worried if she could carry a series,

a valid concern. Those were the days when television was particularly [celebrity] name crazy.

In my research there were to be three spin-offs; any truth to that?
The only one that was really considered was Wonder Girl with Debra Winger. She was wonderful. I think we could have gotten on the air. But Debra announced that she never knew we were thinking about making a spin-off and she wasn't going to do series television. Those where the days when there was a real bias against movie stars coming from television.

Is it true Debra Winger bought herself out of her contract?
I don't think that's true. It was never discussed with me. If she did, it was with Warner Brothers.

How was it working with costume designer Donfeld?
Donfeld was a remarkable costume designer. He really created the look of the show and was brilliant with conceptualizing the Wonder Woman outfit. He worked endless hours. I have known only three designers with that passion and involvement: Donfeld, Nolan Miller for *Dynasty*, and on Broadway, and William Ivey Long for *The Producers*,. Their clothes make a statement.

How did Donfeld feel about being nominated for an Emmy?
He thought it was wonderful. It was hard to take *Wonder Woman* seriously in those days. I have shelves and shelves full of People's Choice Awards, but a handful

of Emmy Awards. It's hard when your shows are so popular.

Is it true that Roy Rogers didn't want Lynda in her Wonder Woman outfit?
I think Roy was at an age when he did the show that she could have worn anything and he wouldn't have cared.

You had a lot of great stars on the series . . .
Batman cast guest stars constantly and that was always kind of one of my fortes. We tried to go after known names in the villain roles as an added enticement. It was a selling point when you didn't have a big star in the lead, but you could dress it up with Cloris Leachman as the mother or Henry Gibson or any of the multitudes of named stars we used.

What ever happened to the fourth season of Wonder Woman?
We made a pitch to CBS with our ideas to update the series by keeping it contemporary, but it didn't work. I thought it got picked up for a half season or something like that, but not a full year.

Did you keep anything from the set?
Some Donfeld sketches of Lynda that he had given to my daughter.

Do you have a favorite episode?
The pilot with Cloris Leachman was my favorite. Leachman was fabulous.

Didn't you model the Dynasty *fight scenes after the fight between Lynda and Stella Stevens?*

I had made a lot of women's prison pictures: *Women in Chains, Women Behind Bars,* and *Cage Without a Key.* Those types of movies always did great numbers and there were always fight scenes with the women. When *Dynasty* was at its peak and the people were saying, "We have gone as far as we can go and done everything we can do," we had a concept meeting one day. They had written a scene with a couple of slaps exchanged. I said, "Why not take it a step further and let's see them get into a knockdown, drag out fight." So, yes, I showed them the fight scene from the pilot between Wonder Woman and Stella Stevens.

The network loved it! Linda [Evans] loved it! The only person who had reservations about it was Joan [Collins] just because Linda was so much stronger than she was. Joan was enough of a showman and she knew what a sensation it could be to see Alexis and Krystal going at it, so she went along with it. But she always dreaded the fights every season because she always ended up black and blue.

The real payoff was when they went out and did "Legends" (a touring play starring Collins and Evans) across country this past winter. Apparently there is a lawsuit pending that Linda was a little too strong on Joan.

Did anyone get hurt during the stunts on Wonder Woman?

Not that I recall. I have always been very careful about stunts and how much you ask of your stars. Lynda always wanted to do a little more than we felt was safe.

You don't want to risk a star you need working five days a week, fourteen hours a day getting injured in a fight or an action sequence. Lynda had a very good stunt woman who looked enough like her to protect her from injury.

How was it working with Lynda on Daddy *in 1991?*
It was terrific for me. It was like going home again. She was great in it and tried very hard. Lynda went through a period where she was a little difficult to work with mainly due to the people that surrounded her at that time. By the time she did *Daddy,* she was coming from a wonderful place: a mother and married. She could not have been more professional.

When she did *Wonder Woman* she was young. She was getting lots of options from lots of people. Often it is very hard for a beautiful young woman who is suddenly hit with stardom to keep everything in place.

I read that Ron Samuels said he was running the set of Wonder Woman?
He was trying to run everything. When it came to Lynda, he wanted to have the final say. There were a number of conflicts and problems. It was not always the happiest of sets.

Lynda Carter and guest looking wonderful at a Washington, D.C. event during a performance of American University's musical troop "PIZZAZ: A Touch of Gold."
(© Mike Pingel)

CHAPTER TWO

After the Cape

Lynda Carter "Diana Prince"

SINCE THE series ended, Carter has starred in the TV movies *Rita Hayworth: The Love Goddess,* and *Danielle Steel's Daddy,* and hit the silver screen in *Sky High* and *The Dukes of Hazzard.*

She continued her singing in five TV specials from 1980 to 1982. She also starred in two short-lived TV series, *Partners in Crime* with Loni Anderson and *Hawkeye.*

In 1982, she divorced her husband/agent Ron Samuels. And in 1984, she married Robert Altman, and she has two children, James and Jessica.

Carter returned to her singing roots in 2005, when she hit the stage in London as the Mama Morton in the West End London production of *Chicago.* She also made TV guest appearances on *Law & Order* and *Smallville.*

In 2008, her independent feature film *Tattered Angel* toured the independent film festival circuit.

Presently, Carter has been touring the United States to sold-out audiences with her own cabaret show. And she has begun working on a new CD, which will be her first since her 1978 LP, *Portrait.* For more on Lynda's concerts, visit www.scottstander.com.

Lyle Waggoner "Steve Trevor"

After *Wonder Woman*, Waggoner went on to guest star on *Murder, She Wrote, Fantasy Island, Happy Days*, and *Mike Hammer*. He also hosted the series, *The Great American Strip-Off*, for the Playboy Channel.

He has been married to Sharon Kennedy since 1961, and has two sons, Jason and Beau.

In 1979, he founded Star Waggons, which is the largest supplier of studio location rental trailers in the entertainment industry.

More recently, Waggoner has made TV guest appearances on *The War at Home*, and *The Love Boat: The Next Wave*.

Saundra Sharp (S. Pearl Sharp) "Eve"

After her partial season on *Wonder Woman*, Sharp continued her acting in *Charlie's Angels, Diff'rent Strokes*, and *T. J. Hooker*. She also had recurring roles on *The White Shadow, St. Elsewhere*, and *Knots Landing*.

In 1980, she cofounded the Black Anti-Defamation Coalition. Sharp is the author of *Black Women for Beginners, On the Sharp Side*, and *Typing in the Dark*. She has also produced several documentaries. For up-to-date information on Sharp, go to www.asharpshow. com.

"Wonder Woman actually stood for something. Besides being glamorous, she stood for peace, love, and equality. She made statements regularly about the strength of sisterhood, and about treating people well. This is something you didn't get from any other female icon. Wonder Woman was the purest embodiment of what a strong woman on television could be."

—Andy Mangels, author

Richard Eastham
"General Blankenship"

After the first season of *Wonder Woman*, Eastham went on to guest star on *The Waltons, Barnaby Jones,*

CELEBRITY QUESTION #1: IF YOU COULD HAVE ONE OF WONDER WOMAN'S SPECIAL ITEMS—BRACELETS, MAGIC LASSO, GOLDEN BELT, GOLDEN TIARA—WHICH ONE WOULD YOU WANT AND WHY?

"I'd take the invisible jet and hire a sexy pilot to fly me around everywhere. Because, come on, who wouldn't want their own private plane?"

—Perez Hilton, gossip gangsta

"I wouldn't pick her magic lasso, that's for sure! As a middle-aged drag queen I am not interested in hearing the truth. I guess her bracelets to fend off all the bullets coming my way from bitter, jealous rivals."

—Jackie Beat, columnist and entertainer

"Wow! Tough decision . . . The bracelets are the most awesome accessory but the golden belt would give me Wonder Woman's power, so I'd pick that."

—Glen Hanson, artist

"Definitely the bracelets. I like the way they seem to be able to stop anything from coming at [me]."
—Reichen Lehmkuhl, actor, *Dante's Cove*

"LASSO. Wrangle up the trash and throw 'em out. See a mugging, lasso the perp, and toss 'em right to the precinct. Just general lassoing all around. Suicide bombers: lasso. President Bush: lasso. Mary Cheney: lasso. Michale Vic: double lasso. You get the picture . . ."
—Julie Goldman, stand-up comedian, *Big Gay Sketch Show*

"Her invisible plane. Who would not want one. It was outrageous!"
—Gabriel Romero, actor, *Dante's Cove*

"I'm not likely to be deflecting bullets at any point in time. I rarely throw anything, other than occasional attitude, so I don't need the tiara, and the belt of strength doesn't give you any muscles, so it would have to be the lasso. Not only did it make people tell the truth but it could actually control their actions. Imagine the possibilities in politics AND the bedroom . . ."
—Andy Mangels, author, *The Wonder Woman Companion*

"Her magic lasso, because then I can lasso any cute guy and bring them to me, heheheh."
—Josh Zuckerman, singer

"My choice is the magic lasso. What better way to wrangle me up a hottie or ten and put 'em in first class aboard the invisible plane? The real wonder about Wonder Woman was the fact that she didn't have guys crawling all over her. They always seemed to be running away!"

—Fernando Ventura, radio host,
Fernando & Greg in the Morning,
energy927fm.com

"Can it be her invisible jet? I've always wanted to join the mile high club in Wonder Woman's invisible jet."

—Allan Brocka, creator of *Rick & Steve*

"Dude. I live in Hollywood. If I could have a magic lasso that makes people tell the truth, my life would be MADE."

—Peter Paige, actor, *Queer as Folk*

"I think definitely the magic lasso. Then I could get the truth out of anyone and any questions I asked I would get the correct answer. Then I could take it off if I wanted to be lied to!"

—Chi Chi LaRue, DJ and director,
Channel 1 Releasing

"I guess I'm just a gullible dumb ass 'cause I believe everyone all the time. I'd love to have that friggin' lasso especially in front of casting directors to see if they really liked me or not."

—Dylan Vox, actor, *The Lair*

"Mmmmm . . . tough question, they're all such fabulous accessories . . . The tiara, of course, would make me feel like a genuine princess . . . the lasso always had a fun and yet kinky vibe . . . and the invisible jet sure would come in handy during L.A. rush hour. But I'd have to go with the belt, since it's the source of all her superhuman strength."

—Craig Taggart, actor, *Sordid Lives: The Series*

"[The Terra] Other than how fabulous it is, I can think of more than a few people I'd like to throw it at! And if I can work it right I could summon a pretty cool robot plane and cut down on cell phone bills to my mom."

—Mark Padilla, artist, GravityFaggot.com

"Only one? Girl, give us the whole damn Wonder Woman wardrobe! But, if we had to choose, it would have to be the truth-extracting magic lasso. What better way to capture someone to pick up the bar tab and find out if he is lying about he and his boyfriend having 'an arrangement.'"

—blog radio hosts, *Fruit Salad*,
fruitsaladshow.com

Galactica 1980, Quincy M.E., and *Dallas.* He also had recurring roles on *Falcon Crest* and *Salvage 1.*

In 2002, Betty Jean, his wife of sixty years, passed away. And three years later in 2005, he passed away due to complications from Alzheimer's.

PARADISE TIPS

In 2008, Lynda Carter made headlines after she found a body floating in the Potomac River while canoeing.

Beatrice Colen "Etta Candy"

Following the first season of *Wonder Woman*, Colen had a recurring role on *Happy Days*. She also worked continuously with guest starring roles on *Alice, CHiPs, Barney Miller, Night Court, Baywatch,* and *Knots Landing.*

She was married to Patrick Cronin and had two sons, James and Charlie. In 1999, Colen passed away from lung cancer.

Lasso of Truth with Producer Leonard Goldberg

Superproducer Leonard Goldberg has produced some of the best TV shows, including *Starsky & Hutch, Family, Charlie's Angels, Hart to Hart, Fantasy Island,* and *T. J. Hooker,* along with a list of many feature films including *War Games, Sleeping with the Enemy, Double Jeopardy, Charlie's Angels,* and *Charlie's Angels: Full Throttle.* Next up, he will be coproducing with Joel Silver the theatrical film version of *Wonder Woman* in conjunction with Warner Brothers and DC Comics.

What drew you to the Wonder Woman project?
I was originally attracted to the project back in the 1970s. I had received the first copy of Gloria Steinem's magazine, *Ms.,* and on the cover was Wonder Woman.

I suddenly started to think about Wonder Woman and thought, here is this an iconic figure that should be done as a movie for young girls. She would be a fantastic character. I was in business with Aaron [Spelling] then and we went about trying to acquire the rights, which were held by DC Comics. We had a deal all set with DC Comics to do it as a motion picture. At that point in time, we had talked to the representatives of the hottest movie star of the day, Raquel Welch, to play Wonder Woman. Then at the last moment our attorneys got a call from DC Comics saying, "We ran it by our sister studio Warner Brothers and they said they were already in the process of developing it as a TV show. They said they had to withdraw."

Ever since then, I always had kept Wonder Woman in the back of my mind. I would talk to Joel [Silver] from time to time about it and he became completely intrigued with the idea. A few years ago Joel said to me, "I managed to get us the rights for Wonder Woman to develop it into a motion picture."

Has it been difficult to find the right actress to play Wonder Woman?
We haven't come to the actress yet. It's been difficult and challenging just to get the right script. We don't want to do a movie just to say, "We're doing a Wonder Woman movie," have a big Friday-night opening, and then have it dissipate quickly because we didn't make a good movie. You only get one shot at handling a legendary figure like Wonder Woman. We want to get it right.

Are you looking at a period piece or more modern?
Frankly, that has been a big discussion. Doing a period piece is a bigger gamble. Any time you do a movie in a specific time period, it's a bigger gamble than doing it contemporary. We haven't made a decision yet.

In terms of the casting, the character will be in her early twenties, and every time a new rumor comes out about the Wonder Woman movie we receive calls from all the agents around town. There are many young actresses who would love to play Wonder Woman. She's a very meaningful character to woman of all ages.

Will it be a mixture of the comic book and TV show?
Both were successful, and the comic books continue to be successful. We certainly want to be respectful of the origins of Wonder Woman, but we are hoping to find our own tone for the movie.

Have you been in touch with your friend Douglas S. Cramer about it?
We talk from time to time, but we've not really discussed Wonder Woman yet, but we will. I just want to have something more specific to discuss with him when we do.

Douglas was my boss when I first joined ABC. He taught me a great deal, not only about the business, but about life. He has been a friend since the 1960s . . . and that's a while ago!

Lynda Carter after her 2007 cabaret show
backstage in San Francisco. (© Mike Pingel)

CHAPTER THREE

Wonder Girl

WONDER WOMAN has a little sister; Drusilla ("Drew" was her big sister's nickname for her) visited her sister a few times during the 1940s in America. She was a curious and whimsical girl, who just LOVED ice cream! The role was played by Debra Winger. Wonder Girl was one of her first roles in the entertainment business. Her raspy voice and cute, good-girl looks made her a perfect choice for the part.

Wonder Girl even had her very own wonder outfit. Her outfit was a bit more understated than her sister's but was still in the red, white, and blue accents. Drusilla also had to twirl when she turned into Wonder Girl.

Wonder Girl was only seen in two episodes during the first season, "The Feminum Mystique, Part 1 and 2" (episodes 5 and 6), and then in "Wonder Woman in Hollywood" (episode 14). Her appearance did make an everlasting impression, not only with the fans but with the studio. It was rumored that they wanted to spin off her character with her own show, and it was also rumored that Debra Winger actually bought herself out of her contract with Warner Brothers because she did not want to do the spin-off show for Wonder Girl.

After *Wonder Woman*, Winger went on to the silver screen in *Urban Cowboy* and *An Officer and a Gentleman*,

The two sides of Wonder Woman drawn by Mark Pallia
(© Mark Pallia) (© CBS/Warner Brothers)

and was nominated twice for an Oscar for her work in *Terms of Endearment* and *Shadowlands*. In 2005, she was nominated for an Emmy for her work in the TV film *Dawn Anna*. In 1982, she took the voice role of E.T. of *E.T.: The Extra-Terrestrial*.

She left the business for a bit, but the Rosanna Arquette documentary *Searching for Debra Winger* was a critically acclaimed look at an aging actress in Hollywood, and was filmed in 2001, the same year Winger returned to the limelight.

In 1993, Winger was a guest on *Late Night with David Letterman* promoting her new film *Wilder Napalm*. At the end of the interview, she tore off her clothing to reveal she was wearing her Wonder Girl outfit underneath and ran through the crowd.

Yet in the eyes of fans, Debra Winger will still and always be that sweet drop-dead-gorgeous little sister of Wonder Woman.

Lasso of Truth
with
Charlene Tilton

It is a little-known fact that I auditioned to be Wonder Girl, Wonder Woman's kid sister. I was approximately sixteen at the time and it was just prior to me starring on *Dallas*. Casting director Mary Goldberg was a big fan of mine and brought me in to meet with the producers. They liked me well enough at that audition that they brought me back to screen test for the part of Drusilla. It came down to me and Debra Winger.

I kept trying to convince the producers that I'm perfect; I'm perfect for the role. Then when I showed up for the screen test, there was obviously a problem. I'm five foot two on a good day and Lynda Carter is six feet tall. She is this tall, statuesque, brunette goddess and I am this short, bubbly, sexy blonde. No one in a million years would believe we were sisters. Debra Winger did her screen test first, and then they put me in one of the Wonder Woman costumes. The crotch came down to my knees and they had to tape it up. I also didn't fill out the top portion of the costume either. They put this hideous black wig on me and told me to read the lines.

I am all dressed and ready to do my audition and Debra Winger walks by me as she was leaving. I just looked at her and said, "Congratulations on becoming Wonder Woman's sister." She looked at me and said, "You haven't even auditioned yet." I said, "Oh look at me. Trust me on this one." I had seen Debra in her Wonder Woman outfit with her dark flowing hair and she was such a wonderful actress anyway. I was positive that she would get it!

They had me do the screen test with someone who was just reading lines to me. Then they had me do the infamous Wonder Woman turn. No matter how well I was able to do that turn, I was not going to get the part. I was so completely wrong. They did like me as an actress with my youthfulness and determination.

I did my best. The physicality just wasn't right and I'm not peculiarly athletic anyway. I can't do all the running around, jumping, leaping, flying, and all that stuff Wonder Woman's sister had to do. It wasn't long after that I got *Dallas*. Things happen the way they are supposed to. I really believe that. I certainly didn't lose any sleep over not getting that part. I knew when I was in that Wonder Woman costume that I was just so wrong for the role. I must have been real cute in that pinned-up costume wearing a mop-top brunette wig with a tiara. I looked like I was a little kid playing dress-up. Hopefully someone burned that screen test!

I would have loved to work with Lynda Carter. She was so good on that show and made it her own. It was a comic book character and she made it very real. She was wonderful in it. She is also an incredible and very talented singer. I have met her since that time, and she is a very lovely woman.

As I reflect back, it was a fun experience, but yes, it was not in the cards for little Charlene. I was definitely more suited to be rolling around in the hay loft with Ray Krebbs.

"Contemporary Wonder Woman" by artist Glen Hanson.
(© glenhanson.com) (© CBS/Warner Brothers)

CHAPTER FOUR

TV's Wonder Woman Effect

Electra Woman and Dyna Girl (1976) – TV Series
This Saturday morning kid show was part of the rotating series on *The Kroft Supershow*. The show starred Deidre Hall as Electra Woman and Judy Strangis as Dyna Girl. It was a combination of Wonder Woman and Wonder Girl with a good twist of Batman thrown in.

They Call Me Bruce (1982) – Theatrical Movie
A parody on Bruce Lee films. The film spoofed the Wonder Woman spin when a character changed in a phone booth and the spinning music was used, minus the explosion.

To Wong Foo, Thanks for Everything! Julie Newmar (1995) – Theatrical Movie
Three drag queens—Noxeema Jackson (Wesley Snipes), Vida Boheme (Patrick Swayze), and Chi-Chi Rodriquez (John Leguizamo)—spin into action as the Wonder Woman theme song plays as they turn a stagnant room into something fabulous!

Spice World (1997) – Theatrical Movie
In this semifictional biography of the girl band, the Spice Girls, tribute is paid to the Amazon goddess as Baby Spice (Emma Bunton) dresses up like the lassoed avenger during a montage that also pays tribute to *Grease* and *Charlie's Angels*.

The Naked Truth: "Hooked on Heroine" (1998) – TV Series
Reporter Nora Wilde (Téa Leoni) dresses up in a Wonder Woman suit. She takes on its persona as it empowers her to tell the truth, aids her in rescuing a dog, and makes her stop thieves from stealing a car. In the end, Lyle Waggoner makes an appearance to buy the suit.

Work With Me: "The Best Policy" (October 6, 1999) – TV Series
Lynda Carter guest starred as herself when one of the show's characters dreamed she was tying him up with the lasso.

The Family Guy: "A Hero Sits Next Door" (1999); "Da Boom" (1999); "Peter's Two Dads" (2007) – TV Series
An animated series that lampoons all things iconic. In "A Hero Sits Next Door," the Super Friends are playing strip poker and Wonder Woman removes her top. In "Da Boom," Twinkie the Kid pretends to be Wonder Woman as a child. Finally, in "Peter's Two Dads," when Peter's mother tells him she does not know who his biological father is, he does a twirl and turns into Wonder Woman.

Electra Woman and Dyna Girl: "Pilot" (2001) – TV Series Pilot

The girls are back in town in this updated version of the seventies show. This time around it starred Markie Post as Electra Woman and Anne Stedman as Dyna Girl. The washed-up, booze-drinking, sex-starved Electra Woman is now living in a trailer court and is pulled out of retirement. Many superheroes are mentioned, and Electra Woman claims that Wonder Woman has better tits even if they are fake.

That '70s Show: "Ramble On" (2002) – TV Series

After Donna (Laura Prepon) buys Eric (Topher Grace) a super-ugly ring, Eric fantasizes that he is Superman and Donna is Wonder Woman, with the rest of the gang as part of the Justice League. At the end of the episode Superman and Wonder Woman make out.

MTV Movie Awards (2002) – TV Special

The opening sequence is a parody of Spider-Man with Jack Black as the webbed crusader and Sarah Michelle Gellar as Mary Jane. While searching for the host of the MTV Movie Awards, Mary Jane spins into Wonder Woman. Eventually they both jump into the invisible plane and fly off to the award show.

The O.C.: "The Best Chrismukkah Ever" (2003) – TV Series

As Summer and Anna both vie for Seth's attention, Summer (Rachel Bilson) dresses up as Wonder Woman as a Christmas gift for Seth (Adam Brody).

The Family Guy Presents: Stewie Griffin: The Untold Story (2005) – DVD Release
As Superman is flying beside Wonder Woman's invisible plane, he finds her sitting on the potty and discovers that she does not wash her hands before returning to the cockpit.

Robot Chicken: "The Real World Metropolis" (2005); "Losin' the Wobble" (2007) – TV Series
Another animated series that lampoons all things iconic. "The Real World Metropolis" has the Justice League living together, with Wonder Woman putting the moves on Batgirl. In "Losin' the Wobble," Wonder Woman (Jordan Ladd), Superman, and The Flash discuss their evil counterparts.

Wonder Woman: Battle of Justice (2005); *Wonder Woman: Balance of Power* (2006) – Feature Films
Two feature films starring Michelle O'Neil as Wonder Woman. In *Battle of Justice,* Wonder Woman is up against corporation corruption. In *Balance of Power,* she picks up where she left off to continue her battle with corruption.

Hustle: "Season 3, Episode 1" (2006, England) – TV Series
After meeting a little boy dressed as Batman, Neal fantasizes about Stacey (Jaime Murray) dressing up like Wonder Woman.

Jimmy Kimmel Live!: "Superhero Hanukkah" (2006) – TV Talk Show
The story of how Hanukkah came to be is reenacted by Wonder Woman (Jennifer Wenger) and additional Hollywood superheroes.

Attack of the Show (2007) – TV Series
A comic skit show that has lampooned the Amazon goddess on several occasions. In its first incarnation, Wonder Woman (Olivia Munn) shows how tough it is being a superhero when your outfit has no pockets and how hard it is to find an invisible plane.

The second time around, in "Wonder Woman's Guide to Office Safety," she (Munn) gives you helpful hints if your office comes under attack by giant squids. And when Munn was away, cohost Kevin Pereira donned the tiara-clad costume showcasing all of Wonder Woman's valuable assets!

Bones: "Mummy in the Maze" (2007) – TV Series
Dr. Temperance "Bones" Brennan (Emily Deschanel) dresses up as the Amazon do-gooder for a Halloween party.

Searching for Wonder Girl (2007) – YouTube Mockumentary by Jesi Kinnevan
A semiserious look at the lack of women superheroes over forty, inspired by the documentary *Searching for Debra Winger*.

PARADISE TIPS

In 2008, Donfeld's rendition of TV's 1970s Wonder Woman costume was on display at The Metropolitan Museum's "Superheroes: Fashion and Fantasy" exhibit. The exhibition featured approximately 60 ensembles, including movie costumes, avant-garde haute couture, and high-performance sportswear.

MINI-LASSO OF TRUTH
WITH JESI KINNEVAN

What was your inspiration to do the short film?
Movies like *Best in Show* and *Drop Dead Gorgeous* were my comedic inspiration. I get a kick out of characters who take themselves too seriously, so I made sure mine were done the same way.

Are you a fan of Wonder Woman and Wonder Girl?
I was a Supergirl fan growing up. However, I knew Debra Winger had played Wonder Girl, so that made it easier to do a spoof on *Searching for Debra Winger*.

How did the film Searching for Debra Winger *impact you?*
It was interesting to hear the perspective of famous actresses on the age issue in Hollywood.

Has your film been shown at festivals? Won any awards?
No festivals. I'm flattered you would think it was that good. It was just my first YouTube video, so I wanted it to be something worth watching.

Playboy (February 2008) – Magazine
Playmate Tiffany Fallon appears on the cover wearing a painted on Wonder Woman outfit for their "Sex in America" issue.

The Wonder Woman Parodies – YouTube Series
Drag queen Brandi Ice takes on the role of a lifetime as she parodies the Amazon icon with comic results in this seven-episode series.

Lasso of Truth
with
S. Pearl Sharp
(aka Saundra Sharp)
as Eve

How was it working with Lynda?
She was very nice. The only drama that really happened was a period when she would not show up for shooting. I was never quite sure what that was about, but it made it a very short day because there was only so much they could do around her.

How was Lyle Waggoner?
He was very very sweet.

How was it working with the IRAC computer?
I remember the board; they were trying to make it look very space age. All those things we take for granted now.

Did the computer really talk?
I think someone was saying the lines offstage and maybe even in a computer voice, I'm not really sure. My thing was, don't forget your lines.

Anything crazy happen on the set?
It was fine until the day they dropped the door on my head! In the show, there's the door that would rise up from the floor and you walk in. I don't know if I paused or the guy rushed that day, but as I walked through, the door came right down on my head. The next thing I knew I was waking up in Lyle Waggoner's arms. I went totally unconscious. I was not sure what had happened. After that, they were afraid I was going to sue and wanted me to go to the doctor. I said "No I'm fine, I don't have time to go through all of that." After that, I couldn't walk through the door and they said, "OK, just come in and we'll edit it later."

What was your favorite episode?
The most interesting show I did was with the actress Judyann Elder, a long-time friend of mine who's actually from my hometown. We were supposed to be the same person, and they made these latex masks for the both of us. When she pulled off her mask, she looked like me, and vice versa. (episode 27, "Light-Fingered Lady")

Did you enjoy being a part of Wonder Woman?
Yes, it was one of the first shows like that I had done. I was not under contract; they just kept calling me back for that part. It was a nice show to work on. The crew was very nice. Just a little drama when she [Lynda] would not show up, but I knew that didn't

have anything to do with me. She was very nice to me when we had a scene together. She was very professional.

One interesting thing about that time in television was that blacks were just beginning to be used in shows. Most of us were working in things like *Good Times, The Jeffersons,* and those kinds of shows. So to have blacks on a show like *Wonder Woman* was kind of a history-making event. Since a lot of the shows were all white, that was a positive thing. It was not about racial casting. Anybody of any race could have played the role that I played. I was glad that representation was there on the show.

What would be a typical day on Wonder Woman?
You come in and do hair and makeup, wardrobe, and all of that. Then there's a read-through with the director and blocking for whatever one or two scenes you're doing. And then you shot it. They didn't spend a lot of time in rehearsal, because by the time I came in, the group was pretty set on how things were going to go. For some reason, my stuff was usually in the morning, particularly if it involved Lynda. We would do those in the morning.

I remember when we were having the short days and I would come in at 6:30–7 AM and pull out around 10 AM After a couple of months, the guard at the gate said, "Where do you work?' and I said, "I work on *Wonder Woman.*" And he said, "I want your job. Every time I see you, you're leaving for the rest of the day."

Did you ever try on the Wonder Woman wig or bracelets? No, none of the above. It would have messed up my 'fro!

Superfan Vicki Mullins dressed in her Wonder Woman
outfit and showing off her lasso and all-American cape!
(© Vicki Mullins)

CHAPTER FIVE

Super Friends Online

Amazon Web Sites!

Lasso over to www.wonderland-site.com;
www.wonderwomancollectors.com;
www.wonderwomanmuseum.com; and
www.wonderwoman-online.com.

To get the most up-to-date info on Lynda's singing
career and tour, go to www.scottstander.com.

For everything new on Wonder Woman, drop by the
DC Comics Web site at www.dccomics.com.

Wonder Woman Day

Andy Mangels has taken his love of Wonder Woman
not only to the World Wide Web and with an upcoming
2009 book, *The Wonder Woman Companion*, but he has
even created "Wonder Woman Day," a yearly charity
event in Portland, Oregon. The event runs the last week-
end of October and raises money for Portland's most
protective domestic violence shelters (largely for women
and children) including Raphael House, Bradley-Angle
House, and the Women's Crisis Line.

AMAZON SPIN WITH MIA CRUZ

Mia Cruz is the owner and official webmistress of www .wonderland-site.com. The site is dedicated to Lynda Carter and all the fans worldwide of Lynda Carter and Wonder Woman.

How many fans visit the wonderland-site.com site?
We get about four to seven thousand monthly.

When did you become a fan of Lynda Carter?
Since I was a kid, very very young. We have quite a bit in common, Lynda and I. In '73, when she was being crowned Miss World USA, I was performing myself in St. Louis.

What was your favorite Lynda Carter show and movie?
I can't answer that because they are all my favorite. Believe me, it's truly hard for me to say that there is one that I could pick over the other because I can identify with so many of them.

What would your favorite episode of Wonder Woman *be?*
OH! I'm probably going to have to say the first episode with all honesty. Just because that was when I first saw it and said, "Oh my God." That's all it took.

Who do you think should step into Lynda's shoes in the new feature film?
I personally think that it should not be somebody famous, seriously. First of all, I really believe it's impossible

for anyone to take the role over. I know they may eventually get somebody, but nobody is going to be able to fill that role the way she has done it. Because Lynda has made it what it is, she pioneered it and nobody is ever going to be able to do that again. They may make a bunch of money off of it, whoever it is, and I hope it becomes a great success. Nobody is really going to be able to fill her shoes.

Do you have a favorite song from her first album?
"Toto" was my favorite one, to be honest. I just love that song.

What is the reaction from the fans with Lynda's CD?
They love it! They are very anxious as we all are to find out when it's going to be coming out.

Why do you feel Lynda was perfect for the role of Wonder Woman?
Believability. She looks the part of what the comic book created. Lynda really made the character believable and everyone can identify with some part of her. Whether you're straight, gay, man, or woman, there are so many people who can identify with her.

What makes it most fulfilling to produce the Wonderland Web site?
Simply stated, it is more than I could ever ask for to be the webmistress and owner of wonderland-site.com for Lynda Carter/Wonder Woman. A dream come true. How cool is that.

AMAZON SPIN
WITH VICKI MULLINS

Vicki Mullins is known around the world as the woman who loves to wonder woman everywhere! See her site at www.geocities.com/wwvicki/.

What is your favorite costume you have created?
Honestly, I like all of them. My most favorite is the original ABC costume, because it's from the very beginning.

Do you only create costumes from the TV show or also from the comic books?
I haven't done any comic costumes. I was looking into making the Cathy Lee Crosby outfit. That is one of the next things I'd like to do.

How long does it take to build one of the costumes?
The original one wasn't more than two months. As we got better with them, they took a little longer because I wanted to add a little more detail.

Which one was the hardest to make?
The one that took the longest was the diving outfit, because it took forever to find the right material.

What is your favorite episode of Wonder Woman?
I have one from when it aired on ABC and one from CBS. The ABC episode is the "Last of the Two-Dollar Bills" because it's the only episode where she takes her tiara off. It's the coolest thing because she can use it as a weapon. From CBS, it's "The Girl from Islandia" be-

cause it's the only episode Wonder Woman cries in. It just touched me.

If you were going to make a new Wonder Woman costume what would it be?
Some sort of a winter outfit. In the comic books sometimes they had her wearing blue jeans and a red shirt with her Wonder Woman gear. Regular clothing would be an interesting twist.

What do you think about the feature film?
I'm looking forward to seeing it and I'm hoping it's going to be a great movie. For me, Lynda Carter is always going to be Wonder Woman regardless of who plays her.

What would you like Wonder Woman to have as a new power or costume in the new film?
I hope they don't make her fly. That was one of the best things about her, that she didn't fly, because she had to do things like normal people, but she still would have extra superhuman power with her magic belt. Keeping it close to that would be really good. They really didn't go into her mental powers in the TV show. Maybe they could explore that a little more.

In the comics, she was always able to make her golden lasso do stuff. She can't control people with her mind, but maybe have them think or remember something when she uses her golden lasso.

What drew you to Wonder Woman?
That she was a woman and that she stood for truth, liberty, and justice. My mom and I use to play Wonder Woman when I was a kid and she reminded me of my mom.

The first Wonder Woman Day in 2006 raised $15,405! In 2007, Wonder Woman Day II was held in Portland and New Jersey; the two combined events raised more than $27,000! In each case, 100 percent of the proceeds was given to charity. Mayor Tom Potter of Portland, Oregon, even declared October 28, 2007, "Wonder Woman Day" to recognize the event's commitment to bringing awareness to domestic violence.

For more info go to www.wonderwomanmuseum .com.

The Music of Lynda

At the young age of fourteen, Carter received her first paycheck ever, for singing with a local Arizona band called Just Us. The band played at a college pub called the Pizza In. When she was seventeen she joined her second band, the Relatives, which traveled a bit, and their first show was at the Sahara Hotel in Vegas. This band-hopping singer took on her last group called the Garfin Gathering with Lynda Carter.

In the early seventies she left the band and returned home. In 1973, she entered and won the Miss World USA pageant. Shortly after that, she was offered to cut two singles, "I Believe in Music" and "It Might As Well Stay Monday."

Then came a little show called *Wonder Woman*, which overnight made Lynda Carter a household name and was as wholesome as all-American apple pie. Carter did find time between all the spins to record her first album, which was titled *Portrait* and was released in

May 1978 through Epic Records, Carter cowrote three of the songs on her album: "Want to Get Beside You," "Fantasy Man," and "Toto (Don't It Feel Like Paradise)".

In August of 1978, Carter opened at Caesar's Palace in Las Vegas, and later in 1980, Carter went on a tour in London with the Johnny Harris Orchestra.

Lynda Live by artist Glen Hanson. (© glenhanson.com)

Carter returned to singing in 2005, when she took on the role of Mama Morton in the musical sensation, *Chicago* at the Adelphi Theatre in London. Carter had not sung on stage in eighteen years. Carter also performs "When You're Good to Mama" on the *Chicago* tenth anniversary CD release.

In May 2007, she premiered in her own cabaret act at the Plush Room in San Francisco to sell-out shows. She has begun to tour America with her critically acclaimed cabaret. For more on her appearances go to www.scottstander.com.

Lynda Carter's Specials

Lynda Carter's Special, CBS, January 12, 1980. Guest Stars: Kenny Rogers, Leo Sayer

Lynda Carter Encore!, September 16, 1980. Guest Stars: Merle Haggard, Tom Jones, John Phillips, Donald Young

Lynda Carter Celebration, May 11, 1981. Guest Stars: Ray Charles, Jerry Reed, Chris Evert-Lloyd. Awards: Walter Painter won the Emmy for Outstanding Achievement in Choreography and the show was nominated for Outstanding Art Direction for a Variety or Music Program.

Lynda Carter: Street Life, March 5, 1982. Guest Stars: George Benson, Tony Orlando, Frank Stallone. Awards: Emmy nominated for Outstanding Technical Direction and Electronic Camerawork.

Lynda Carter Body and Soul, March 16, 1985. Guest Stars: Eddie Rabbitt, Ben Vereen. Awards: Emmy Award nominations: Outstanding Art Direction for a

CELEBRITY QUESTION #2: WHAT WAS YOUR FAVORITE *WONDER WOMAN* EPISODE AND WHY?

"I always loved any episode with her little sister or when she would go back to the island where she came from. It would just change the dynamics of the show, in a really fun way."

—Perez Hilton, gossip gangsta

"'My Teenage Idol Is Missing' from season 3, of course! And the reason why can be explained with just two words: LEIF GARRETT!"

—Jackie Beat, columnist and entertainer

"Bar none . . . 'The Feminum Mystique.' Lynda at her most stunning, Debra Winger as Wonder Girl, Carolyn Jones as the Queen, Hot John Saxon, Nazis on Paradise Island, Wonder Woman racing down the airstrip, grabbing the plane wing and flicking hair out of her face . . . what's not to LOVE!"

—Glen Hanson, artist, glenhanson.com

"I liked the one where she went back to the 'mother island' and there were a bunch of other 'wonder women' there. Maybe there were more than one like that, but hey that's my favorite Wonder Woman memory."

—Reichen Lehmkuhl, actor, *Dante's Cove*

"I can't really remember any of the specific Wonder Woman episodes. I may not be a good candidate— except I loved Lyle Waggoner, and wished I looked like him, and Wonder Woman would want to date me."

—Julie Goldman, stand-up comedian, *Big Gay Sketch Show*, julie-goldman.com

"I can't remember a specific one, but I always loved it when the other Amazons were around. I mean, a whole island full of sexy, tough yet docile, scantily clad, horseback-riding warrior women was almost too much fun for my pubescent mind."

—Gabriel Romero, actor, *Dante's Cove*, gabrielromero.com

"My favorite Wonder Woman episode was the two-part 'The Feminum Mystique', because it has the perfect melding of Wonder Woman mythology from the comics . . . even though they named Drusilla incorrectly, and they should have been mining for Amazonium, not Feminum. Other than those changes, it covered every aspect of Wonder Woman mythology from the 1940 comics: it had her mother, it had Wonder Girl, the invisible plane, Paradise Island, and all the Amazons. The only thing it didn't have was the

Kangas (large kangaroo-like creatures) that the Amazons ride in the comic books."

—Andy Mangels, author,
The Wonder Woman Companion

"I like the episode where Wonder Woman goes up against a magician who has discovered a way to turn lead into gold."

—Josh Zuckerman, singer, joshzuckerman.com

"There is one episode where Wonder Woman battles a searing hot, pervert laser that hits her square in the boobs each and every time! Luckily, she is quite the gymnast and somersaults above the laser several times before finally delivering the knockout blow by deflecting the pervert laser with her bracelets. Oh how I coveted those bracelets only a little less than the magic lasso. But with my luck, those things would've deflected men as well as bullets."

—Fernando Ventura,
Fernando & Greg in the Morning

"My favorite *Wonder Woman* episode is the one where 'Diana Prince' goes undercover as 'Diana Paradise' in a beauty contest. It's so terribly campy and rather evil. When Diana first suggests that she infiltrate the beauty pageant, Steve's response is 'Thanks Diana, but I'm afraid this calls for a really gorgeous girl.' And as if that wasn't bad enough, he adds, "Someone who looks great in a bathing suit.' When Diana does manage to get into the contest, much to Steve's shock, the biggest compliment he'll give her is 'Seeing you in that dress makes me realize you look like somebody.' 'Who?' she asks. It hits him. 'Joan Crawford.' Eventually Wonder Woman wins the contest and she wasn't even in it. She just leaped onto the stage to save someone's life. She then runs off to rescue General Eisenhower and Steve, but manages to get back for the end of the contest just to collect the prize. Steve muses how terribly ashamed Diana must have felt even to be seen on the stage with someone as gorgeous as Wonder Woman."

—Allan Brocka, creator, *Rick & Steve*

"It's been a long time, but I always loved it when they went to Paradise Island. And when Wonder Woman went diving in the ocean that looked almost exactly like a swimming pool. I'll tell you what episode I DIDN'T like—the pilot. I watched that thing a couple years ago and it's AWFUL."

—Peter Paige, actor, *Queer as Folk*, peterpaige.net

"I don't know if I have a favorite, but I always liked the ones when women guest stars came on, like Stella Stevens, Linda Day George, and Joan Van Ark."

—Chi Chi LaRue, DJ and director,
Channel 1 Releasing

"I loved the episode with Wonder Girl played by bitchy Debra Winger. The two women together was just too silly to be believed and if you add Morticia Addams into the mix [Carolyn Jones] it was a campy nightmare come true."

—Dylan Vox, actor, *The Lair*, dylanvox.com/

"It's hard for me to isolate one particular episode—as I still get giddy every time I see Diana Prince twirl into a huge fireball—but I remember reeeeeally wanting to be 'The Boy Who Knew Her Secret'. That was a plot line that, even as a four-and-a-half-year-old, appealed to me. To be in on the secret; what kid didn't want that? My rationale at that age was, I suppose: 'If I couldn't be HER, at least I could be her friend.' Granted, that didn't stop me from TRYING to be her . . ."

—Craig Taggart, actor, *Sordid Lives: The Series*

" 'Wonder Woman Meets Baroness Von Gunther' from ABC's season 1 forties era. I think that episode really sums up some of the show's best qualities, like how Wonder Woman handles small children with such care, and the absolutely great ending with a catfight that has the baroness fall in the pool and then get read by Wondy: 'I hope you'll learn from your unwomanly mistakes.' SNAP!"

—Mark Padilla, artist, GravityFaggot.com

"Season three's 'Amazon Hot Wax'. That's the episode where our fabulous superheroine goes undercover as a singer trying to nab the evildoers in the recording industry. So, not only does she fight crime, but Wonder Woman also belts out a few tunes (with her real voice, might we add) to boot. It is SO musical theater! A must see! We think she sounds like Karen Carpenter."

—blog radio hosts, *Fruit Salad*

"Wonder Woman had an across-the-board audience. Straight men and lesbians wanted her to be their girl-friend. Straight women wanted her as their best friend or protector. Gay men wanted her to be their older sister, their friend, and a mother figure; they recog-nized that she stood for equality for everyone, and for love and peace. She did not care what you did as long as you treated each other with kindness and you stood up for people. Even young gay people going through their struggle of being gay recognize the need for people who feel that way."

—Andy Mangels, author, andymangels.com

Variety or Music Program, Outstanding Lightning Direction for a Limited Series or Special, Outstanding Technical Direction, Camerawork, Video for a Limited Series or a Special.

The Fans' Favorite Song!

To this day, Lynda Carter fans' most favorite song is "Toto," which Carter wrote about the struggles in show business. The song is requested every time Carter performs live. She also sang the song in "Amazon Hot Wax" (episode 52), and during 2008 she began to include the song in her cabaret act with new lyrics.

CELEBRITY QUESTION #3: DO YOU REMEMBER WHEN AND WITH WHOM YOU FIRST WATCHED *WONDER WOMAN*?

"By myself. In my room."

—Perez Hilton, gossip gangsta, perezhilton.com

"I watched the pilot episode with my sister Vicki on Friday, November 7, 1975. We probably ate Swanson TV dinners with diet Shasta black cherry soda in our pajamas."

—Jackie Beat, columnist and entertainer, jackiebeatrules.com

"In 1976, sitting on green shag carpeting with my father watching the pilot movie. I will never forget it."

—Glen Hanson, artist, glenhanson.com

"With my best friend Jason. We were five years old. After each show, I would tape strips of dark construction paper to the back of his and my head and make capes out of towels in the closet and we would run around the house. Oh, and I had the bracelets too, made out of tin foil. Jason didn't get the bracelets. Only I was allowed to wear those. LOL."

—Reichen Lehmkuhl, actor, *Dante's Cove*, reichen.us

"I first watched Wonder Woman in elementary school. I thought she was awesome, but couldn't understand why she was wearing a bathing suit; I always thought she'd be comfortable in pants and sneakers. In general, lady superheroes always look like strippers or professional swimmers. Wonder Woman could also have a name like Titties McGee, Super Boob Stripper Lady, or Titsy Von Snatch—strong and powerful till the right mayan (man said with a ma-y-an) comes along. The guys always have tight suits—yes—but they're covered and don't have to wear high heels. Perhaps she could have like, Spandex pants or shorts, a huge camel toe, knee-high boot/sneakers, a reinforced sports bra/tank top, and a tattoo that says F YOU. That would be wondrous. Truly, truly wondrous."

—Julie Goldman, stand-up comedian,
Big Gay Sketch Show

"I watched *Wonder Woman* in Mexico City with my brothers. Dubbed into Spanish it was even more surreal. You should try it."

—Gabriel Romero, actor, *Dante's Cove*

"I found out it was coming on the air and I did extra chores for a week. I lived in a little town in Montana and we only got one TV channel and it was not ABC. We could get ABC from Washington, but you had to have a super duper TV with great antennas on it to get the signal. We borrowed our neighbor's color television so I could watch the debut on television. It was one of the defining elements of my youth. I watched it with my parents. We were Mormons. My dad very much appreciated the beauty and grace of Lynda Carter. My mom very much appreciated the femininity and strength of Lynda Carter. I appreciated all of it!"

—Andy Mangels, author,
The Wonder Woman Companion

"I think it was my mom."

—Josh Zuckerman, singer

"Probably with my sister who hated Wonder Woman. But I screamed and made a fuss and eventually had my way. My sister eventually became a prostitute. If she had recognized Wonder Woman as a positive female role model, her life could've been different. Let that be a lesson to all of you."

—Fernando Ventura,
Fernando & Greg in the Morning

"I first watched *Wonder Woman* by myself after school in second grade. I kept thinking if I could spin around fast enough, and hold my wrists at the exact same angle, maybe I'd turn into something too."

—Allan Brocka, creator, *Rick & Steve*

"I'm sure I watched it alone. One of the great challenges of my early life was playing superheroes with my friends and having to be The Flash because I was a boy."

—Peter Paige, actor, *Queer as Folk*

"Yes, with my friend Kevin, who was Lynda Carter obsessed, who had her record, had the Wonder Woman doll, and when Lynda was a special guest on TV specials we always had to tune in. The first time I watched *Wonder Woman* was with him."

—Chi Chi LaRue, DJ and porn queen

"The first time I saw the show was in reruns on TNT or Nick at Nite I think. My brothers and sisters and I had a male babysitter who loved the show and we used to run around the house acting like we had magical powers. He was cute too . . . Damn, I wonder whatever happened to him."

—Dylan Vox, actor, *The Lair*

"Although, I don't remember my actual 'first' *Wonder Woman* . . . I do know that I don't remember life before *Wonder Woman*. I just remember it being a Friday night RITUAL during '77–'79. One of my earliest memories is laying on the vinyl floor of my aunt's house . . . her making Jiffy Pop and me glued to the TV set, anxiously awaiting the opening credits. (speaking of which: is there, to date, anything on television more amazing than the opening credits of season 3 *Wonder Woman*?)"

—Craig Taggart, actor, *Sordid Lives: The Series*

"My earliest memory of watching the show was when I was about four years old: *Wonder Woman* would always come on at 5 PM, right when my mom got home from work. It was a pretty climactic end to the day for me at that age. My mom would watch the show with me and we would draw Wonder Woman together—that was how I began to learn to draw. It's a favorite memory of mine."

—Mark Padilla, artist, GravityFaggot.com

"Yes and it's still the hot topic at therapy. This event could have single-handedly lent to us becoming the FRUIT-tastic homosexuals we are."

—blog radio hosts, *Fruit Salad*

Lasso of Truth with Stella Stevens, Episode #1: "Pilot: The New Original Wonder Woman"

How was it wearing those great outfits?
I really loved it, especially the snood—you know, where they wore the hairnets to hold all the abundant long hair at that time and all the other hair puffed out at the front, like bangs that were very curly. That was a good one; I hadn't worn a snood before.

How was the director, Leonard Horn?
I love the man who was the director. He died shortly after filming the pilot. They never had his touch again. I don't think it would have been as good a movie without him. They had tried another pilot and it failed. They got him and it ran for two or three years, and it ran without me. I was just a bad girl in the first one.

I wish that the director had lived longer so I could have worked with him again, because he was wonderful.

How was it being the bad girl?
Wonderful. Wonderful! I don't get to do that much in real life. It was great and the meaner and more slant-eyed I got the better, I thought. All the good girls have big

bright eyes and the all the bad girls had thin skinny eyes. All Nazi, all the time, oh how silly!

She was all evil so she had to play totally innocent. That's mainly what I did, tried to be as sweet and gentle and congenial as possible, so no one would ever think I was a spy!

How was working with the great Red Buttons?
Red Buttons I adored. It was so fun to work with him, he was my cohort too.

How was it to work with Lyle Waggoner?
Lyle is just a dream. He loves to work. He's a gentleman and he loves to joke with his fellow actors and he's always just on the top of everything. He knew his lines, he knew what he was going to do. He had a pretty good take on this person he was playing. I thought it couldn't have been done better.

How about working with Lynda Carter?
Lynda was great. She was fun to work with and worked very hard. She was very sweet and nice to me. We had such fun when we had that fight. She did not get hurt nor did I and we didn't have stunt doubles do very much of anything. We did most everything of it. They just came and told us what was going to happen. Like when the chandelier falls with me, she just jumps and swings on it and it's fine and I do it and the thing falls! [laughing]

We had wonderful stunt people who taught us some of the things we did as we were fighting. It wasn't so much like a girly fight, it was a good fight. These guys were the top stunt doubles for a lot of western films.

We all had such fun, everyone huddled about watching us if they could. It took about two hours at the most to shoot. Everything went smoothly and it was a lot of fun.

Lynda seemed to be made for the role and everyone helped her a great deal. She did not seem insecure at all, if she felt afraid, then she hid it graciously. She's our fearless leader, she is Wonder Woman.

What about your character?
It was a lot of fun. Just doing the period thing and wearing silly clothing like that. It really helps your characters; you don't see people walking around with their hair up in snoods as much. Her behavior was pretty bad, but they couldn't tell she was the spy, that's what I couldn't get. Why don't they know this! [laughing] What's the secret?!

What did you enjoy most about doing the film?
Well, I was so proud of how well it turned out, and the fact it did go to a show, even though I was not in it. That means it was a great success. It was one of the most fun things I have ever done. To see the director giggling with laughter when you're done, you know you've done something real well and everyone else will too. He's going to be the hardest judge of all.

I would have loved to have been a villainess who could stand to come back but I never was. I guess I was too memorable as the Nazi spy!

"Golden Age Wonder Woman" by artist Glen Hanson.
(© glenhanson.com) (© CBS/Warner Brothers)

CHAPTER SIX

The Episodes

Season 1
Wonder Woman
Network: ABC
Years: 1975–1977

The pilot and the first few episodes ran as specials. The series was finally put into a regular time slot for ABC-TV in December 1976. After thirteen episodes, and a successful run, ABC-TV decided to cancel the series.

Episode #1 — Pilot: "The New Original Wonder Woman"
Airdate: November 7, 1975
Writer: Stanley Ralph Ross
Director: Leonard Horn

The opening images set the theme in the summer of 1942 when President Roosevelt and Prime Minister Churchill were trying to fend off Hitler and his Nazi crusade from their attempts to take over the world. The narrator lets the audience know that the only hope for freedom and democracy is Wonder Woman.

The Nazis plan to bomb a Brooklyn naval yard by

air. Major Steve Trevor makes plans to intercept the Nazi plane over the Bermuda Triangle before it can reach its U.S. destination. During the mission, Steve is wounded and is found unconscious on the uncharted Paradise Island, home to an immortal race of Amazons. Diana, an Amazon princess, ends up developing an unconscious attraction to Steve.

While being nursed back to health by Diana and the island doctor, they learn about the Nazis and their worldwide threat. The Amazon queen holds a special tournament of athletic games to determine which of her Amazons will return Steve to the outside world and assist in his fight against the Nazis. After the competition ends, the winner removes her disguise and it's revealed to be Diana.

As Diana prepares to enter the outside world, the queen gives her a red, white, and blue costume that has a removable skirt and stands for her allegiance to freedom and democracy; a golden belt that will help her retain her cunning strength while she is away from Paradise Island; and a golden lasso that is indestructible and compels people to tell the truth. The queen reminds her daughter that in the world of ordinary mortals she is a "wonder woman." And with Steve by her side, they fly back to Washington in Diana's invisible plane.

Back in the United States, as Steve recovers, he is made aware of a new plan by the Nazis to make another bomb attack. But before he can do anything about it, he is kidnapped and drugged. Diana, now as Wonder Woman, discovers what is happening and intercepts the Nazi plane and crashes it into a Nazi submarine. Afterward, she goes back to rescue Steve and informs him of what has developed. Steve, totally enamored with Wonder Woman, thanks her for her assistance.

A few days later, General Blankenship introduces Steve to his new and ordinary secretary Yeomen First Class Diana Prince (Wonder Woman's alter persona).

Wonder Guest Stars

Cloris Leachman "Queen Hippolyta"
Funny lady Leachman is well known for her work as Phyllis Lindstrom on the *Mary Tyler Moore Show*, which won her two Emmys for the role, and for the spin-off series *Phyllis*, for which she won a Golden Globe. Her feature films include *Young Frankenstein, High Anxiety, Spanglish*, and the upcoming 2008 film *The Women*. In 1971, she won the Oscar for Best Actress in a Supporting Role for *The Last Picture Show*.

Stella Stevens "Marsha"
In 1960, Stevens won a Golden Globe for Most Promising Newcomer. She went on to appear in the films *Li'l Abner, Girls! Girls! Girls!, The Courtship of Eddie's Father, The Nutty Professor*, and *The Poseidon Adventure*. She has also been inducted as an official member of the Stuntman Academy.

John Randolph "General Phil Blankenship"
Randolph has also appeared in *All the President's Men, King Kong*, and more recently in *You've Got Mail*. He won a Tony Award as Best Actor for *Broadway Bound* in 1987.

Red Buttons "Ashley Norman/Carl"
Buttons is best known as a stand-up comic in his own show, *The Red Buttons Show*, during the fifties. He went

on to win an Oscar for Best Actor in a Supporting Role for *Sayonara* in 1957. And in the 1990s, he received an Emmy nomination for his appearance on *E.R.*

Gregory Harrison "First Lieutenant of the Army Medical Corps"
Harrison went on to play in TV's *Logan Run* and *Trapper John M.D.*. He also played a male stripper in *For Ladies Only* and a gay man whose boyfriend is stricken with AIDS in *It's My Party*.

Eric Braeden "Captain Drangel"
Braeden is best known for his ongoing role as Victor Newman on the soap opera *The Young and the Restless,* for the last twenty-eight years. He also makes a second guest appearance on *Wonder Woman* in "Skateboard Wizard" (episode 44).

Lasso Tips

When the pilot originally aired, the opening credits listed it as *The New Original Wonder Woman.* However, when it was released to DVD/video, the title was changed to *Wonder Woman.*

The Amazons are immortal on Paradise Island. If they left, they would revert to being mortal.

The queen mentions that Diana is her only child.

Diana competes in disguise as Amazon XXXIII.

Steve Trevor's safe combination is 24L 36R 33L.

Marsha, Steve Trevor's secretary, is a Nuremberg judo champ, lives at 2809 W 20th Street in Chevy Chase, Maryland. And her phone number is CAPITOL-6732.

"The pilot was extraordinarily written by Stanley Ralph Ross. The dialogue is almost straight from the 1940s comic books. The Wonder Woman pilot is the truest and most faithful representation that Hollywood has EVER done of a comic book.

"Wonder Woman had a unique element to it because although Lynda Carter was a beautiful actress, as Wonder Woman she was not threatening to anyone in the audience."

—Andy Mangels

WW Toys

Wonder Woman can mimic any person's voice.

Wonder Woman is able to deflect bullets from a machine gun firing at her.

Episode #2: "Wonder Woman Meets Baroness Von Gunther"

Airdate: April 21, 1976
Writer: Margaret Armen
Director: Barry Crane

A top Nazi spy ring is at work again in Washington and General Blankenship is afraid that Steve's life might be in danger since he was responsible for putting their leader, Baroness Von Gunther, in prison. After several shipments of top-secret weapons are sabotaged, Steve is falsely accused by the FBI of being a spy, and it's up to a young amateur sleuth and Wonder Woman to clear Steve's name and maintain his war-hero status.

Lasso Tips

In the Wonder Woman comics, Baroness Von Gunther's first name was Paula, and she was a blonde.

In order for her climb the side of the prison, Wonder Woman's lasso is able to increase in length.

Arthur Deal drives a 1939 Packard with license plate number 23-605. He lives at 8 Estate Dr., Arlington. And his estate is most recognizable as the home of Mr. Hart in the 1980 big-screen hit, *9 to 5*.

Actor Richard Eastham takes over the role as General Blankenship in this episode.

WW Toys

Wonder Woman can mimic General Blankenship's voice.
Wonder Woman uses her lasso to save Tommy and to
   capture the baroness.

Cat Fight
Wonder Woman and Baroness Von Gunther go claw to
claw, ending with the baroness landing in a pool.

Comic Crossover
In the comic books, Baroness Von Gunther is one of
Wonder Woman's most notorious nemeses. At one point
Wonder Woman reforms the baroness of her evil ways.

Episode #3: "Fausta, the Nazi Wonder Woman"

Airdate: April 28, 1976
Writers: Bruce Shelley and David Ketchum
Director: Barry Crane
   Wonder Woman's Nazi counterpart, Fausta Grables,
captures Wonder Woman and brings her to Germany

PARADISE TIPS

There were not many connections between the series and
the original comic book villains, but the seventies TV
series did have an effect on the story lines in the comics.
During the first season of the series, DC Comics created
a line of Wonder Woman comics that returned to the
1940s to mirror what was happening on the series.

so she can learn the secret of her strength. Steve sneaks into Germany to rescue her and at the same time obtains information on who some of the double agents are. Eventually Wonder Woman is able to escape due to the ignorance of the chauvinistic Nazi men.

Lasso Tips

This is the first episode that had General Blankenship's secretary Etta Candy as an integral part of helping in the adventure.

When Steve goes off to Germany, he sends Diana a note to tell her to take some time off. He signs the note, "Steve," which would be considered very taboo for the 1940s.

Lynda Day George's (Fausta) real-life husband Christopher George guest stars in this episode as "Rojak."

Fausta masquerades as Wonder Woman in an identical outfit that includes a cape and a golden mask.

WW Toys

After Wonder Woman is captured, her lasso is used on her to find out how her mystical powers work.

Wonder Woman mimics General Blankenship's voice once again.

Comic Crossover

Fausta Grables is one of Wonder Woman's comic book nemeses.

Episode #4: "Beauty on Parade"
Airdate: October 13, 1976
Writer: Ron Friedman
Director: Richard Kinon

A string of accidents at four military bases seem to be a sabotage plan against a top-secret radar scanner. The only connection is Jack Wood's Miss G.I. Dream Girl beauty contest, which Diana decides to infiltrate and becomes one of the contestants. Steve eventually figures out that the sabotaged radar project and the beauty contest were the Nazi's plan to distract them from the real crime: the assassination of General Eisenhower.

Lasso Tips

Due to the expense and time it took to film the slow-motion transformation of Diana into Wonder Woman, the light/explosion were added to speed things up. And her street clothes totally disappear during the change.

When Diana decides to enter the beauty contest as "Diana Paradise" wearing a red wig, Steve totally slams Diana's appearance by telling her that beauty contests are for pretty women.

Steve thinks Diana looks like Joan Crawford, around the ankles.

Wonder Woman takes home the title of Miss G.I. Dream Girl.

WW Toys

Wonder Woman uses her lasso to climb a side of a
building.
Wonder Woman uses her superstrength to throw a
telephone pole and a bomb.

Wonder Guest Stars
Anne Francis "Lola Flynn"
Francis is a former Miss America beauty and won a
Golden Globe for her portrayal of the lead character in
the self-titled TV series *Honey West*. She also costarred
in *Funny Girl* with Barbra Streisand.

Christa Helm "Rita"
Helm was known as the Playboy Bunny who dated Joe
Namath, Warren Beatty, Desi Arnaz Jr., and George
Hamilton. However, she became known as the Black
Dahlia of the 1970s after her tragic murder. Even to
this day, the mystery of her death has not been
solved.

Dick Van Patten "Jack Wood"
Van Patten is best remembered for his fatherly role in
the hit TV series *Eight is Enough*.

Episode #5: "The Feminum Mystique, Part 1"
Airdate: November 6, 1976
Teleplay: Jimmy Sangster
Story: Barbara Avedon and Barbara Corday
Director: Herb Wallerstein

Queen Hippolyta sends Drusilla (Wonder Woman's kid sister) to the United States to bring Diana back to Paradise Island so she can assume the throne. Believing that she is Wonder Woman, the Nazis kidnap Drusilla/Wonder Girl so they can discover the secret of her strength.

Lasso Tips

This is the first episode where we meet Wonder Woman's kid sister, Drusilla / Wonder Girl.
The queen teaches Drusilla how to "spin" herself into Wonder Girl.

WW Toys

Wonder Girl uses her superstrength to throw bad guys.
Wonder Woman uses her bracelets to fend off gunfire.

Wonder Guest Stars

Debra Winger "Drusilla/Wonder Girl"
Winger went on to be nominated for three Oscars for her work in *An Officer and a Gentlemen, Terms of Endearment,* and *Shadowlands.* In 2005 she was nominated for an Emmy for her work in *Dawn Anna.*

Carolyn Jones "Queen Hippolyta"
Jones is best known as Morticia Addams in 1960s TV series *The Addams Family.* She was also nominated for an Oscar for Best Actress in a Supporting Role for 1957's film *The Bachelor Party.*

Episode #6: "The Feminum Mystique, Part 2"

Airdate: November 8, 1976
Teleplay: Jimmy Sangster
Story: Barbara Avedon and Barbara Corday
Director: Herb Wallerstein

After discovering that "Feminum" is the secret to Drusilla/Wonder Girl's strength, the Nazis trick her into telling them where Paradise Island is located so they can harvest this rare metal for themselves. Fearing for her Amazon sisters, Diana rushes back to Paradise Island to help them reclaim their homeland and save their immortal secret.

Lasso Tips

Paradise Island coordinates are 30.22 degrees north and 64.47 degrees west.
The Hybirdna Tree, which can only be found on Paradise Island, has the ability to erase human memory.
Amazon women are immortal.
Captain Radl (John Saxon) shows off his bare chest.

WW Toys

Wonder Woman whips out her lasso to wrestle information from Nazi leader Captain Radl.
Wonder Woman and Wonder Girl use their super-strength to throw bad guys.
Wonder Girl uses her bracelets to fend off bullets.

Episode #7: "Wonder Woman vs. Gargantua!"

Airdate: December 18, 1976
Writers: David Ketchum and Tony DiMarco
Director: Charles R. Rondeau

The Nazis have trained a great ape to kidnap and kill Wonder Woman. When the two finally encounter each other, Gargantua goes in for the kill. However, Wonder Woman refuses to hurt him due to her extreme devotion to animals. As she befriends him, Wonder Woman helps the beast to understand and stop his destructive ways and eventually releases him back into the wild.

Lasso Tips

The photo of Wonder Woman from "Beauty on Parade" is used to assist in the deprogramming of Gargantua.
Wonder Woman violates one of the commandments of Paradise Island in this episode by mentioning Paradise Island to Steve and the scientist.

WW Toys

Wonder Woman uses her lasso to climb the side of a building and to tie up a Nazi doctor.
Wonder Woman uses her bracelets to save Gargantua.

Wonder Guest Stars

Robert Loggia "Hans Eichler"

Loggia was nominated for an Oscar for his work in the film *Jagged Edge*. More recently, he has made several appearances on the hit cable TV series *The Sopranos*.

John Hillerman "Conrad Steigler"
Hillerman is best known as Jonathan Quayle Higgins III in *Magnum, P.I.* and starred in the feature films *Paper Moon, What's Up, Doc?*, and *The Last Picture Show.*

Mickey Morton "Gargantua"
Morton went on to appear as 'Malla' Mallatobuck in *The Star Wars Holiday Special* and played Drill Thrall Kloog in the TV series *Star Trek.*

Episode #8: "The Pluto File"
Airdate: December 25, 1976
Writer: Herbert Bermann
Director: Herb Wallerstein

A mercenary known as "The Falcon," arrives in Washington, and steals the Pluto File, which contains information on how to duplicate natural earthquakes. The Falcon then proceeds to use this data to set a series of explosions around a nuclear power plant in order to turn Washington, D.C. into a huge time bomb. Wonder Woman, with the assistance of the creator of the Pluto File, devises a formula that will prevent the disaster from happening.

Lasso Tips

Diana has an uncanny ability to see through hospital walls as she notices The Falcon is trying to shoot the professor from the building across the street.

Diana also makes a blunder by turning into Wonder Woman in the same hospital room in front of the professor, but she also does this in front of the window that The Falcon is trying to shoot the professor through.

As Steve and Diana are visiting a man stricken with the bubonic plague, they are both masked even though they have both already been inoculated for the plague. Yet the nurse attending to the young man is unmasked.

Wonder Guest Stars

Robert Reed "The Falcon"

Reed is best remembered for his good-guy image as Mike Brady of the *The Brady Bunch*. Reed passed away from AIDS-related complications in the early 1990s.

Hayden Rorke "Professor Warren"

Rorke is well known as Dr. Alfred E. Bellows from *I Dream of Jeannie*. He also appeared on the silver screen in *An American in Paris* and *Pillow Talk*.

Episode #9: "Last of the Two-Dollar Bills"

Airdate: January 8, 1977

Writer: Paul Dubov and Gwen Bagni

Director: Stuart Margolin

Top Nazi agents undergo plastic surgery to become look-alikes of high-ranking government employees in order to infiltrate the United States Bureau of Printing and Engraving. Their goal is to steal the engraving plates of the $2 bill in order to cripple the U.S. economy with billions of counterfeit bills.

Lasso Tips

Diana and Etta eat at the Capitol Café.

Steve defuses a bomb.

Nazi agent Wotan, posing as a photographer, charges
    fifty cents for candid photos.
When Steve is brought down to the café basement,
    watch for the shadow of the boom mike in the top left
    corner of the screen.

WW Toys

Wonder Woman stops a car and breaks a lock with her
    bare hands.
Wonder Woman uses her tiara to bust a hole in the
    Nazi's raft.
Wonder Woman mimics a secret agent's voice to alert
    Steve, even though she has not met the agent yet.
Wonder Woman wears her seldom-seen cape and skirt.

Historical Fact

The $2 bill has been around since 1862 and was discon-
tinued in 1966. Ten years later in 1976, it was reissued
and has been in circulation since. Even though it is not
commonly used, it does make up approximately 1 percent of the current U.S. currency.

Episode #10: "Judgment from Outer Space — Part I"

Airdate: January 15, 1977
Writer: Stephen Kandel
Director: Alan Crosland

The Council of Planets considers the inhabitants of
Earth as savages and they want to sterilize the planet.
Before deciding the fate of the world, they send Andros
down to find any reason that they should not go ahead

with their plans. Wonder Woman meets up with Andros, befriends him, and attempts to show him that humans are worth saving.

Lasso Tips

Etta has the "hots" over the Nazi spy who is using her to obtain top-secret information.
The president assigns a "Strike Force" to keep tabs on Andros and to kill him if necessary.
Diana and Steve have their first major disagreement.

WW Toys

Wonder Woman uses her lasso on Andros to make sure that he has been telling the truth.
In order to enter Andros's spaceship, Wonder Woman mimics his specific whistling sound.
Wonder Woman has the power to heal herself after she is gassed.

Flying Fashions
Wonder Woman is once again seen wearing her cape and skirt.

Episode #11: "Judgment from Outer Space — Part II"
Airdate: January 17, 1977
Writer: Stephen Kandel
Director: Alan Crosland

After Andros is kidnapped by the Nazis, he begins to understand the Americans' fight for freedom. When

Wonder Woman unselfishly comes to his rescue, Andros learns that she is the hope for the human race and for the entire planet. Due to her actions, the Council of Planets decides to give the Earth fifty years to become a civilized race. And Andros looks forward to seeing Wonder Woman again in 1992.

Lasso Tips

The photo of Wonder Woman from "Beauty on Parade" is used to assist in determining if the kidnapped agent really is Wonder Woman.

Steve becomes jealous over Wonder Woman's infatuation with Andros.

Wonder Woman turns down Andros's invitation to experience a thousand different galaxies because she knows her efforts are needed here on Earth.

WW Toys

Using her superstrength, Wonder Woman turns steel doors into a barrier to block the Nazis.

Episode #12: "Formula 407"

Airdate: January 22, 1977
Writer: Elroy Schwartz
Director: Herb Wallerstein

An Argentine professor has created a formula that makes tires as strong as steel. He is neutral regarding the war and wants to give the formula to the United States. Steve and Diana go to Buenos Aires to obtain the formula and protect it from falling into the hands of the Nazis.

Lasso Tips

Diana is told that she'd be a very attractive lady if only
 she would remove her glasses and change her drastic
 hairstyle.
Yeoman Prince speaks fluent Spanish.

WW Toys

Wonder Woman uses her superstrength to pull over a
 shelf full of wine even though Steve was unable to
 make it budge.
Wonder Woman is able to catch bombs in midair.

Episode #13: "The Bushwhackers"

Airdate: January 29, 1977
Writer: Skip Webster
Director: Stuart Margolin

In an effort to destroy the war efforts, cattle rustlers are
stealing stock from the military's largest supplier of beef.
Steve and Wonder Woman make their way to the Dia-
mond Ranch in Texas to investigate. They soon discover
that the owner's young son has been supplying inside information to the rustlers in retaliation for the lack of attention from his father after he adopted five war orphans.

Lasso Tips

Steve Trevor's airplane tail number is 93.
Wonder Woman is caught sashaying around in her cape.
In order to go country-western, Wonder Woman turns in
 her usual outfit for a low-cut red top with long sleeves

BEST DIANA
PRINCE COVERS!

Diana as Wonder Woman poses as an actress dressed up as Wonder Woman in "The Piped Piper" (episode 20).

Just ring for maid service and Diana will come running in "The Queen and the Thief" (episode 21).

Showing off her singing abilities, Diana croons songs in "Amazon Hot Wax" (episode 52). Remarkably, she sounds a lot like actress/singer Lynda Carter!

After letting her hair down, literally, Diana joins a dating service in "A Date with Doomsday" (episode 54). It's uncanny how she has a resemblance to Wonder Woman, yet no one notices.

and white pants. However, she still accentuates her outfit with her belt, lasso, tiara, and those stunning bracelets.

WW Toys

Wonder Woman uses her superstrength to bend bars and to push a boulder.

Wonder Woman's magic lasso is used to help Steve climb out of a hole.

The orphans uses Wonder Woman's golden belt to break down the jail door with a wooden pole.

Wonder Guest Stars

Roy Rogers "J. P. Rogers"

Rogers is well known for his 1950s TV shows *The Roy Rogers Show* and *The Roy Rogers & Dale Evans Show*.

Lance Kerwin "Jeff"
Kerwin is best known as the lead character James Hunter in the 1970s TV series *James at 15.*

Episode #14: "Wonder Woman in Hollywood"

Airdate: February 16, 1977
Writer: Jimmy Sangster
Director: Bruce Bilson

The War Department gives their approval to a new Hollywood picture based on four real-life war heroes, including Steve Trevor. Soon, all four war heroes are kidnapped, and it's up to Wonder Woman and her visiting sister Drusilla to rescue them and help a "not-so-brave" corporal regain some of his confidence.

Lasso Tips

Diana is the future heir to the throne of Paradise Island.
Paradise Island is celebrating its 2,000th anniversary.
This episode marks the final appearance of Wonder Woman's kid sister Drusilla.
This is the final episode for Major Steve Trevor, General Blankenship, and Private Etta Candy.

WW Toys

Wonder Woman uses her lasso to get the truth
Wonder Woman uses her superstrength to throw two bad guys.
Wonder Girl's bracelet is used to deflect bullets.

Wonder Girl uses her superstrength to throw four bad guys and runs beside her sister.

Invisible Plane
Wonder Girl is flying the invisible plane to America.

Wonder Guest Stars
Debra Winger "Drusilla/Wonder Girl"
This is Winger's second and final appearance as Drusilla/Wonder Girl.

Carolyn Jones "Queen Hippolyta"
This also notes Jones' second and final appearance as the Amazon queen.

Robert Hays "Jim Ames"
Hays is best known as Ted Striker in the films *Airplane* and *Airplane II: The Sequel*. He has also been the voice of Iron Man/Anthony "Tony" Stark in two animated TV series, *The Marvel Action Hour: Iron Man* and *Spider-Man*.

Season 2
The New Adventures of Wonder Woman
Network: CBS-TV
Years: 1977–1978

After its cancellation by ABC-TV, *Wonder Woman* was quickly picked up by CBS-TV. In its transition to a new network, the series theme changed too. Instead of being set in the 1940s, it was now taking place in modern time. Diana would work with Steve Trevor's look-alike son for the IADC and be more independent than before.

Episode #15: "The Return of Wonder Woman" (ninety-minute movie)

Airdate: September 16, 1977
Writer: Stephen Kandel
Director: Alan Crosland

Steve Trevor and a group of scientists and engineers are flying over the Bermuda Triangle when their plane gets hijacked by a terrorist working for Dr. Solano. After everyone gets knocked out by sleeping gas, the plane spirals out of control and is intercepted by the magnetic field of Paradise Island.

When the plane lands, everyone aboard is still passed out. Diana boards to check on the people and finds Steve Trevor. Puzzled over this, she brings him to the island doctor only to find out that he is Steve Trevor Jr., the son of the man she worked for thirty-five years ago in 1942. While under light hypnosis, Steve reveals what transpired on the plane. Alarmed by what she has heard, Diana feels that she should go back and protect America. The Amazon council holds a special election and they all vote in favor for Diana to return; but she is challenged by her cousin with the competition of "bullets and bracelets."

After winning the competition, Diana is reminded by her mother that without her costume and accessories she is just an ordinary woman. The island doctor proceeds to implant into Steve's subconscious the acceptance of Diana as his new assistant. Still asleep, Steve and the group are returned back to the plane and it is put back up in the air where it began its initial descent. Wonder Woman wakes them up using a special flute and then quickly boards her invisible plane to begin her life as Steve's assistant.

During Diana's first assignment, Steve gets abducted by Dr. Solano's men and is replaced by a double. Later, at the air force base meeting, the imposter Steve gives orders for the delivery of a nuclear power plant to a secluded area picked out by Dr. Solano. When Wonder Woman realizes that the fake Steve is an imposter, she rescues the real Steve and they set forth to capture Dr. Solano and have the nuclear power plant rerouted to its original destination.

Lasso Tips

Steve's associate has just quit to get married.
The queen gives Diana some Tetra Drachma to sell for money.
Paradise Island has a magnetic field that can pull planes down to the ground.
Wonder Woman mentions that she is 2,527 years old on her next birthday.
IRA the computer makes its first appearance.

WW Toys

Wonder Woman's outfit gets an updated look. The bracelets are now gold to match her belt and tiara. The lasso will still make people tell the truth, but it can also be used to erase their memories.

Wonder Woman is able to contact her mother on
  Paradise Island through the ruby in her tiara.
Wonder Woman shows off her moves during a fight
  with Gloria.

Wonder Guest Stars
Beatrice Straight "The Queen"
Straight is best known for her role in *Poltergeist*. She
also won an Oscar for Best Actress in a Supporting Role
for her work in the 1976 film *Network*.

Episode #16: "Anschluss '77"
Airdate: September 23, 1977
Writer: Dallas L. Barnes
Director: Alan Crosland
    A high-ranking former Nazi official is trying to re-
create the movement, which is referred to as Anschluss
'77. Steve and Diana go to South America and discover
that Nazi doctors are working on cloning Adolf Hitler.

Lasso Tips

Wonder Woman is on the cover of *Tempo* magazine
  with the caption WONDER WOMAN RETURNS.
Diana and Steve receive their assignments from a
  computer that signals them by flashing lights that
  make a beeping sound.

WW Toys

Wonder Woman grips the bottom of a helicopter and
  stops a tank with her hands.

Wonder Woman heals Steve Trevor's shoulder with
finger acupressure.

Episode #17: "The Man Who Could Move the World"

Airdate: September 30, 1977
Writer: Judy Burns
Director: Bob Kelljan

A Japanese man blames Wonder Woman for the
death of his brother during World War II. Seeking vengeance, he uses a brain-wave amplifier machine to force
her to walk through a minefield similar to the one he
believes his brother was killed in. After short-circuiting
the amplifier with her own personal will, Wonder
Woman reunites the man with his long-lost brother.

Lasso Tips

Watch for a shameless plug of the Wonder Woman doll
    with Wonder mentioning that it's a collectors item
    and that only a few were sold for charity during
    World War II. In reality, this doll was produced by
    Mego Toys in 1976.

WW Toys

In the 1940s flashback scene, while Wonder Woman is
    rescuing two boys from a minefield, she is wearing
    the updated seventies version of her outfit.
Wonder Woman flies her invisible plane.

"I think it's an excellent representation of what Wonder Woman was intended to be. She shows sympathy, empathy, and also regret for actions that caused harm to somebody. She tries to defuse a violent situation by talking about how important peace is and how violence does not solve anything. She doesn't use violence herself, and that's rare for a superhero.

"What other show is going to tackle the Japanese internment camps in any fashion other than a documentary. To use this as a plot element on a superhero show and have it make sense—and work—was brilliant. It was the best written episode of the series."

—Andy Mangels

Episode #18: "The Bermuda Triangle Crisis"

Airdate: October 7, 1977
Writer: Calvin Clements Jr.
Director: Seymour Robbie

A new U.S. military nuclear test site located within the Bermuda Triangle is being sabotaged. Diana fears that if something goes wrong, it could easily destroy Paradise Island. As Steve and Diana investigate, they realize that the man behind the attacks has created a "Stingray" submarine in order to begin his plan of controlling the world.

Lasso Tips

The "Seaview" submarine from the film *Voyage to the Bottom of the Sea* doubles as the "Stingray" submarine.

The nuclear test site is actually the Point Vicente Lighthouse located in Rancho Palos Verdes, California.

The coordinates given for Manta's island are the same as those mentioned for Paradise Island in "The Feminum Mystique, Part 1" (episode 6).

WW Toys

After Steve crash-lands into a tree, Wonder Woman uses her superstrength to lower him to the ground.

In order to keep in contact with her queen mother, Wonder Woman rubs the ruby of her tiara.

Diana turns her ripped pants into a pair of dazzling short shorts by cutting the legs off with a knife.

Wonder Fashion!
Wonder Woman sports her full-body aqua outfit.

Episode #19: "Knockout"
Airdate: October 14, 1977
Writer: Mark Rodgers
Director: Seymour Robbie

A terrorist group known as "The Movement" kidnaps Steve and makes an attempt on Diana as they infiltrate the World Trade Conference. Their objective is take government leaders hostage in order to make demands to improve the world.

Lasso Tips

A light flashes to let Diana know that she needs to answer the red phone hotline, which is directly linked to the IADC.

The Camden Hotel (now the Los Angeles Airport

Marriott by LAX) was used to film a portion of this episode. The hotel is also used in "Stolen Faces" (episode 46) and "Spaced Out" (episode 50).

One of the captions states that it is 11:15 PM, but when they show the hotel, it's in complete daylight.

One of the recycled spins from this episode is not edited well since she is wearing a skirt but spins wearing jeans.

WW Toys

Wonder Woman uses her tiara to knock a gun out of the bad guy's hand.

Wonder Woman blocks gunfire using her bracelets.

Comic Crossover

Carolyn Hamilton in "Knockout" (episode 19) is loosely based on the comic book character "Nubia." Nubia only appeared in two issues of Wonder Woman comics in the early seventies and was a black Amazon sister who had been separated from her at birth.

Wonder Guest Stars

Ted Shackelford "Peter 'Pete' Johnson"

Shackelford makes a second appearance in "Time Bomb" (episode 43). In this episode he works with Joan Van Ark, who ended up playing his TV wife on the long-running TV series *Knots Landing*. Shackelford is currently appearing in the daytime serial *The Young and the Restless*.

STEVE TREVOR ALL TIED UP!

Episode #2: "Fausta, The Nazi Wonder Woman" – Steve is tied up and placed in a box. All he needs is an address to be delivered to!

Episode #12: "Formula 407" – Steve is tied up in the wine cellar with an unconscious, tied-up Wonder Woman and he does not make his move on her. Very interesting; he just might be . . .

Episode #14: "Wonder Woman in Hollywood" – Steve is tied up and gagged in a van with three other guys. Now this sounds like a hot film you might pick up in a video store's back room.

Episode #15: "The Return of Wonder Woman" – Steve is handcuffed to a weight machine. Now you do see that every day at the gym.

Episode #19: "Knockout" – Steve is tied up and hung in a warehouse as a prisoner of The Movement. Now that is one hanging piece of prime beefcake.

Jayne Kennedy "Carolyn Hamilton"
Kennedy was crowned Miss Ohio in 1970. She was considered as a possible replacement for Kate Jackson on *Charlie's Angels*. She went on to be the first black actress on the cover of *Playboy* and became one of the first female sports announcers.

Episode #20: "The Pied Piper"

Airdate: October 21, 1977

Writers: David Ketchum, Tony DiMarco, and Brian McKay

Story By: David Ketchum and Tony DiMarco

Director: Alan Crosland

Joe and Diana fly to Los Angeles in search of Joe's troubled daughter Elena, who has become prey to the hypnotic charms of flute player Hamlin Rule. Under Rule's spell, Elena becomes his involuntary accomplice in stealing his concert receipts, using a device he created that can transform steel into dust.

Lasso Tips

When Diana is tied to a chair, she is still able to spin around to turn into Wonder Woman.

WW Toys

Wonder Woman throws a heavy speaker using her superstrength.

Wonder Woman uses the heel of her boot to stop a rotating chair.

Wonder Woman deflects bullets with her bracelets.

In order to infiltrate Hamlin Rule's compound, Wonder Woman is disguised as herself (Wonder Woman) to easily sneak past the guards.

Wonder Guest Stars

Eve Plumb "Elena Atkinson"

Eve Plumb is best known for her work as Jan Brady in

The Brady Bunch. More recently she has made appearances on *That '70s Show* and the daytime serial *All My Children.*

Comic Crossover
Hamlin Rule—"The Pied Piper"—was a villain of The Flash in the comic book series.

Episode #21: "The Queen and the Thief"
Airdate: October 28, 1977
Writer: Bruce Shelly
Director: Jack Arnold

Diana goes undercover as a maid to protect a queen and her jewels from an international jewel thief who is masquerading as an agent pretending to be a count. Wonder Woman informs the queen that she has been deceived by this man, and that Steve is the real agent sent in to protect her jewels. When the jewels turn up missing, it leads them back to the person who originally hired the jewel thief, the queen's ambassador.

Lasso Tips

Diana becomes a domestic by pretending to be a maid.

WW Toys

When summoned by the IADC to come to work, Diana turns into Wonder Woman in order to get to work faster.

Wonder Woman uses her tiara to knock a gun out of the hand of a bad guy.

Episode #22: "I Do, I Do"

Airdate: November 11, 1977
Writer: Richard Carr
Director: Herb Wallenstein

When Diana masquerades as the new wife of the president's assistant, they are followed as they travel to a health resort in Arizona. While there, Diana hopes to become the next target of the resort owner, who gathers information from the wives of top Washington officials in order to sell it to the highest bidder.

Lasso Tips

This is the first time that Diana takes off her glasses throughout most of the assignment.
First time Diana has a pony tail.

WW Toys

Wonder Woman throws tires, stops a golf cart, and picks up a car with her hands.

Episode #23: "The Man Who Made Volcanoes"

Airdate: November 18, 1977
Teleplay: Brian McKay and Dan Ullman
Story: Wilton Denmark
Director: Alan Crosland

An ex-government professor has developed a ray beam that can create volcanoes. He wants peace throughout the world and if nation superpowers do not disarm

THE OPENING SONG

The song and the opening credits had everyone watching mesmerized! For the first season, comic storyboards brought Wonder Woman alive on the TV screen. The opening sequences had a unique charm when comic book characters became real, live people and Wonder Woman's eyes and Steve Trevor's teeth twinkled.

When the show flew into the seventies, so did the music, with a more upbeat disco sound, and the opening sequences began to contain live-action footage from the series.

their weapons of mass destruction he will turn the entire planet into a volcano. Diana is sent in along with additional agents to stop him. As the beam is initiated, Wonder Woman intercepts it using her body as a barrier to save the world.

Lasso Tips

The opening credits have changed to live action and theme music has been synthesized.

Joe Atkinson has been promoted and Steve Trevor will be handing out the assignments.

Diana and Mei Ling have a major cat fight. Can we say "kung fu fighting!"

WW Toys

Wonder Woman used her bracelets to deflect bullets.
Wonder Woman picks a man up, smashes through a
   stone wall, and uses her body to stop the laser
   beam.

Wonder Guest Stars
Roddy McDowall "Professor Arthur Chapman"
McDowell also appeared in the episode "The Fine Art
of Crime" (episode 40). He is known for his work in the
TV show *Batman* and such films as *Cleopatra*, *Planet of
the Apes*, and *Fright Night*.

Roger Davis "Jack Corbin"
Davis is well known for being the first husband of *Charlie's Angels* star Jaclyn Smith. He was also known for his
work on *Dark Shadows* (costarring with Kate Jackson)
and *Alias Smith and Jones*.

Episode #24: "Mind Stealers from Outer Space, Part 1"
Airdate: December 2, 1977
Writer: Stephen Kandel
Director: Michael Caffey

Andros returns to Earth to help Wonder Woman
save the planet from the Skrill, who have come to harvest human minds and sell them to other civilizations
in the galaxy. When the Skrill discover that Diana
Prince is Wonder Woman, they unleash Zardor (a Darth
Vader wannabe) to capture her mind.

Lasso Tips

Andros was originally played by Tim O'Connor in
"Judgment from Outer Space" (episodes 10 and 11).
The Planetary Council refer to Earth as "Terra."
Diana sees double trouble when she fights twins who
have been taken over by the Skrill.

WW Toys

Wonder Woman pulls a police car out of a ditch.

Wonder Guest Stars
Dack Rambo "Andros"
Rambo is best known for playing a recurring role as
Jack Ewing on *Dallas*.

Anne Ramsey "School Bus Driver"
Ramsey is best known for her work in *The Goonies* and
was nominated for an Oscar for Best Actress in a Supporting Role for *Throw Momma from the Train*.

Vince Van Patten "Johnny"
Van Patten went on to play the Bionic Boy. He currently
is a commentator for the *Poker World Tour* and was in
the film *Deal*.

Episode #25: "Mind Stealers from Outer Space, Part 2"
Airdate: December 9, 1977
Writer: Stephen Kandel
Director: Alan Crosland

With less than forty-eight hours, Andros has to capture the Skrill or the Planetary Council will unleash a frequency that will make two million earthlings slip into madness. During a United Nations meeting conducted by Andros, the Skrill invade the conference and capture his mind. Wonder Woman eventually apprehends the Skrill, and returns the stolen "minds" to their original owners.

Lasso Tips

This episode contains the most Wonder Woman spins, including five spins.

Andros still has a crush on Wonder Woman and asks her to leave the Earth for a second time.

Steve has a new secretary named Eve.

The IRA computer now assists Diana and Steve with their cases.

WW Toys

Wonder Woman makes a shelter out of metal beams in a collapsing building and pushes an oak desk across the room.

Wonder Woman uses her bracelets to deflect the Skrills' death rays.

Episode #26: "The Deadly Toys" (The Holiday Episode)
Airdate: December 30, 1977
Writer: Anne Collins
Story by: Carry Wilber
Director: Dick Moder

One of three scientists who are working on the XYZ project is replaced by a look-alike human android that self-destructs during a board meeting. When the second scientist meets with the same fate, the IADC puts the third one in a safe house. The one person, place, or thing that they have in common are the toy soldiers they play with from a local toy store. After Diana investigates the toy store, a model toy plane attempts to dispose of her. Diana soon surmises that Major Dexter, who brought this to the IADC's attention, is working with the toy manufacturer to sell the XYZ project to a foreign country. Wonder Woman pulls a switch and lets the androids be sent to the foreign market instead of the real scientists.

Lasso Tips

When Steve asks IRA what to get Diana for Christmas, the computer refers to her as Wonder Woman.

WW Toys

Wonder Woman uses her tiara as a boomerang.
Wonder Woman kicks open a door.
Wonder Woman fights an android version of herself.

Wonder Guest Stars
Frank Gorshin "Dr. Hoffman"
Gorshin is best known for his work as the Riddler on the TV show *Batman,* for which he also earned an Emmy nomination. He also made appearances on *Star Trek* and *Charlie's Angels.*

Episode #27: "Light-Fingered Lady"

Airdate: January 6, 1978
Writer: Bruce Shelly
Director: Alan Crosland

Diana goes undercover as a crook to capture a master thief who is planning a heist of fifty million dollars. Hidden in a sarcophagus, Diana is delivered inside the place of action. As she turns into Wonder Woman, she deactivates the alarm and subdues the dog so that she can let her accomplices in. However, the security team resets the alarm, which Diana accidentally trips. The thieves leave her inside to be the fall guy, but Wonder Woman outsmarts them and Diana and Steve catch the bunch red handed.

Lasso Tips

The shot of the Los Angeles Police Department is similar to the one used in the TV series *Charlie's Angels* and *Police Woman*.

This marks the first time we see Steve's new assistant Eve.

Lynda Carter as Wonder Woman actually flips Bubba Smith over her shoulder in this episode!

WW Toys

Wonder Woman uses her bracelets to disarm the alarm system.

Wonder Woman uses her lasso on the guard to lead her to the file room and has him forget she was at the warehouse.

Wonder Woman uses her mind powers in order to speak to the guard dogs so that they will not attack her or the other thieves.

Wonder Woman sports her full-body aqua outfit.

Wonder Guest Stars

Christopher Stone "Tony Ryan"

Stone is best known for his work in the horror films *The Hollowing* and *Cujo,* and was married to Dee Wallace, the mom from *E.T.*

Bubba Smith "Paul Rojak"

Smith is a football player turned actor. During his football career he played for the Baltimore Colts, Oakland Raiders, and Houston Oilers He is best known for his work in the *Police Academy* films.

Episode #28: "Screaming Javelin"

Airdate: January 20, 1978

Writer: Brian McKay

Director: Michael Caffey

Marion Mariposa is kidnapping top athletes in order to have his country win the Olympics. IRA tells Diana who the next possible victim will be. As Diana goes to guard the athletes, they all get captured and she is used as bait in order to make Wonder Woman complete his winning Olympic team. In the end, Wonder Woman ends up freeing the athletes while Mariposa disappears.

THOSE WHO KNEW HER SECRET

Only a handful knew that Diana Prince was really Wonder Woman in disguise:

At IADC, both the supercomputer IRA and Rover knew. IRA, which analyzes all the data, determined that Diana Prince was also Wonder Woman. He kept that ultra TOP SECRET.

Andros, the man from outer space who saved Earth twice, saw right through Diana's disguise! There was more than just saving the planet behind his motives; he was also in love with her in "Judgment from Outer Space" (episodes 11 and 12) and "Mind Stealers from Outer Space" (episodes 24 and 25).

Those pesky Skrills who came down to Earth to harvest the human minds find out her secret too in "Mind Stealers from Outer Space."

The Leprechaun might have a pot of gold, but he also admitted to Diana Prince that he knew we all have "secrets" in "Pot of Gold" (episode 47)!

The only real person to know her secret was Skip in "The Boy Who Knew Her Secret" (episodes 56 and 57). As an evil alien hiding on planet Earth, the fake Cameron also knew her secret and almost got away with erasing Diana's memory of who she really was.

He's no stupid ape: Gargantua knew her secret, but who was he going to tell in "Wonder Woman vs. Gargantua!" (episode 7)?

Lasso Tips

The last time Diana saw Mariposa, she thought he had
drowned in the North Sea.
Wonder Woman mentions she fought Napoleon.

WW Toys

Wonder Woman throws a bomb into the air and bends
jail bars.
Wonder Woman uses her tiara as a boomerang.

Wonder Guest Stars

Rick Springfield "Tom Hamilton"
Springfield also appears in "Amazon Hot Wax" (episode
52). He is best known as Noah Drake in the daytime series *General Hospital*. Springfield is also a very successful
recording artist and won a Grammy for "Jessie's Girl."

Ron Callard "Bill Bethude"
Callard is a well-known bodybuilder who won the titles
Mr. USA in 1975, Mr. America in 1977, and Mr. Inter-
national in 1978.

Episode #29: "Diana's Disappearing Act"
Airdate: February 3, 1978
Writer: S. S. Schweitzer
Director: Michael Caffey

Defying the laws of nature, a magician is able to turn
base metals into gold. At the same time, Diana mysteriously receives a gold pendant without any explana-
tion. The magic it holds is that it's slowly turning back

into lead. The magician is trying to cash in on a ten-million-dollar con to exchange his newly made gold for oil in order to cripple the world's economy.

WW Toys

Wonder Woman throws a briefcase of explosives into the air, cracks open a safe, and breaks through a brick wall.

Wonder Woman uses her bracelets to deflect bullets.

Wonder Guest Stars

Ed Begley Jr. "Harold Farnum"
Begley is best known for his Emmy-nominated role in *St. Elsewhere*. More recently, he has had recurring roles on *Veronica Mars, Six Feet Under, Boston Legal,* and *CSI: Miami.*

Comic Book Crossover

"Morgana" was a Wonder Woman villain in the comic book, but was not portrayed the same in the TV series.

Cross Dress Alert Episode—Episode #30: "Death in Disguise"

Airdate: February 10, 1978
Writer: Tom Sawyer
Director: Alan Crosland

A telegram gives Diana and Steve a lead that assassin Woodward Nightingale is about to strike, and the wealthy playboy Carlo Indrezzano seems to be the target. A second hit man is sent in posing as a female major in order to gain access to the IADC computer IRAC. Their goal is to destroy the computer system before it can expose the plan to kill Indrezzano and leave his partner in charge of his empire.

Lasso Tips

The Hacienda Health Spa is revisited. It was last seen in episode "I Do, I Do"(episode 22).

Diana's apartment is #210.

WW Toys

Wonder Woman catches a man as he falls out of a tree she is shaking. She also stops a car, lifts a dump truck, and pulls a shotgun in half to tie up the bad guy with.

Wonder Woman uses her lasso with instructions to make the person stay immobile.

Wonder Woman is able to run forty-seven miles in less than four minutes.

Wonder Woman uses her superhearing in order to detect a bomb.

Wonder Guest Stars

George Chakiris "Carlo Indrezzano"

Chakiris is best known for his role as Bernardo in the film *West Side Story*, for which he won the Oscar for Best Actor in a Supporting Role in 1962.

Charles Pierce "Starker/Finlay"

Pierce was a well-known female impersonator. He has performed as Bette Davis, Mae West, Tallulah Bankhead, Gloria Swanson, and Joan Crawford.

Jennifer Darling "Violet Louise Tree"
Darling is best known as playing Peggy Callahan on the
TV series *The Six Million Dollar Man* and *The Bionic
Woman*.

Episode #31: "I.R.A.C. Is Missing"

Airdate: February 17, 1978
Writer: Anne Collins
Director: Alexander Singer

After a top computer system has been robbed of its
data, the IADC is called in to investigate. According to
IRA, the next system to be robbed is the power company, and the third will be IRA's. After unsuccessful
attempts to stop these robberies, it's up to Wonder
Woman and Rover, a new roving computer module, to
find the thieves and recover the stolen computer information.

Lasso Tips

Rover, a talking roving computer, becomes the newest
    member of the IADC.
The voice of IRA, the computer system, changes.
IRA shares with Diana that he knows her "secret."

WW Toys

Wonder Woman uses her lasso to find the truth and
    deactivate a bomb.
Wonder Woman catches a falling man.
Wonder Woman uses her bracelets to deflect red lasers.

CELEBRITY QUESTION #4: WHICH WONDER WOMAN OUTFIT WOULD YOU WANT TO WEAR RIGHT NOW AND WHY? THE 1940S CLASSIC OUTFIT? THE 1976 UPDATED OUTFIT? MOTORCYCLE OUTFIT? COUNTRY-WESTERN OUTFIT? OR THE AQUA OUTFIT?

"I'd make my own version!"
—Perez Hilton, gossip gangsta, prezehilton.com

"Uh, which one would cover a plethora of figure flaws? I really love that 1976 number, but I might get lucky if I wore the motorcycle outfit!"
—Jackie Beat, columnist and entertainer, jackiebeatrules.com

"How do you know I'm NOT wearing this outfit right now? 1977 updated costume with the cape!"
—Glen Hanson, artist, glenhanson.com

"I like the aqua outfit; it's very sleek and timeless."
—Reichen Lehmkuhl, actor,
Dante's Cove, reichen.us

"Clearly I would have to make my own. But the motorcycle look is a good start."
—Julie Goldman, stand-up comedian,
Big Gay Sketch Show, julie-goldman.com

"No, my friend, I would not look good let alone fit in an outfit like that. Perhaps the tailored suits she had to wear as a disguise . . . but then I'd look like Flounder Woman, or some hairy cha-cha working at the Pentagon!"
—Gabriel Romero, actor, *Dante's Cove*,
gabrielromero.com

"Either of the traditional outfits would help me suck in my gut. However, given I tend to like leather, I probably would have to choose the motorcycle outfit, which is the Wonder Wet Suit with the helmet added to it. Not only could she twirl around into that outfit but there was always a motorcycle handy for her to jump onto. That's a great power to have."
—Andy Mangels, author, *The Wonder Woman Companion*, andymangels.com

"The classic outfit for sure . . . because there is something to be said about the original classic look of Wonder Woman."
—Josh Zuckerman, singer, joshzuckerman.com

"Well, the seventies look is so out once again so that's not an option. With even Jessica Simpson making a country album, the honky-tonk Wonder Woman ensemble is très chic! But I have to pick the aqua outfit. If all of the world is waiting for you, then you better be outfitted for travel across the ocean. And when Wonder Woman arrives, she doesn't have time to wait for her satin tights to clean in the delicates cycle. Waterproof and quick drying is the way to go!"

—Fernando Ventura, *Fernando & Greg in the Morning*, energy927fm.com

"The seventies outfit. No contest. It's the boots."

—Allan Brocka, creator, *Rick & Steve*, ricksteves.com

"I'm all about the 1976 outfit redux—sexy yet classic. Plus I have good legs."

—Peter Paige, actor, *Queer as Folk*, peterpaige.net

"I think I like the aqua outfit the best, because it's the sluttiest and has the most French-cut crotch. I like sluttier, more boobs, more cleavage, and the thinner the band of fabric over the crotch the better."

—Chi Chi LaRue, DJ and director, channel1releasing.com

"The skateboard outfit, of course. It was basically the regular outfit with some crazy felt boots and that horrible safety hat which always cracked me up. I mean, she's Wonder Woman! Why the hell does she need the safety hat? What is the point of being Wonder Woman if you can't even fall off a skateboard without getting hurt?"

—Dylan Vox, actor, *The Lair*, dylanvox.com

"The updated '77 CBS outfit for sure. It was skimpier, flashier, and sexier but it never made her look cheap. Drag queens and gay men across the world are still asking, "'What's her secret?'"

—Craig Taggart, actor,
Sordid Lives: The Series

"Definitely the 1976 TV version designed by Donfeld. It was the year I was born and I really think that outfit

Episode #32: "Flight to Oblivion"
Airdate: March 3, 1978
Writer: Patrick Mathews
Director: Alan Crosland

Diana goes undercover as a staff sergeant and photo-journalist to investigate the sabotage of several air force bases. A new air force test plane, the Z-400, is believed to be the next target. Diana's first photo assignment is to cover a music group that is arriving on the base to perform. The group's manager, a former army colonel, has turned enemy agent and uses hypnotism on several base staff. Steve Trevor is caught and held captive on the in particular would look most flattering on my figure and show off the most chest hair!"

—Mark Padilla, artist, GravityFaggot.com

"Please give me the aqua outfit!! If you look as gorgeous as Lynda Carter, you need to be prepared for the wet and wild. ;-)"

—Rico, blog radio host, *Fruit Salad*, fruitsaladshow.com

"1976 all the way. I like that the shorts got shorter as time evolved, but I still think it is the defining Wonder Woman costume. I swear I would wear that costume every day. Grocery shopping, at the gym, fighting crime . . ."

—Pauly, blog radio host, *Fruit Salad*, fruitsaladshow.com

tour bus, but Wonder Woman comes to his rescue, uses her magic lasso on the manager to uncover his plan, and stops the sabotage event.

Lasso Tips

There are two spins in this episode and one and a half are done by an obvious body double.

WW Toys

Wonder Woman jumps onto the wing of the plane, up the sides of buildings, and then jumps to the top of a tower.

Wonder Woman throws explosives off the tower and stops a bus with her hands.

Wonder Woman uses her bracelets to deflect bullets. She also uses them to create the sound of a bell in order to break a hypnotic spell.

Episode #33: "Séance of Terror"

Airdate: March 10, 1978
Writer: Bruce Shelly
Director: Dick Moder

Diana is attending a peace conference in which a young boy with psychic powers takes individual pictures of three diplomats with an instant camera. When the pictures develop, a departed family also appears in the photograph with them. Using the photos, the boy leads the diplomats back to his home where his aunt and uncle plan to trick them into pulling out of the conference.

Lasso Tips

IRA admits he knows that Diana Prince is Wonder Woman.

Diana poses as Ms. Carol Littleton, a rich woman who wants to find the "spirit" of her late son Jason.

WW Toys

Wonder Woman bends a pipe into a wall.

GUEST STAR MEMORIES: KRES MERSKY "THEODORA"

How was it working with Lynda?
Lynda was very sweet and beautiful. I remember everyone thinking how gorgeous she was in her little outfit and I don't believe the crew was allowed to leer. [laughs] She was completely professional and very nice to work with.

Any crazy things happen on the set?
Not really, but that smoke machine made us sick! I do remember Lynda had some minor surgery during that episode which put her out for a while so we all got paid for a month. That was very nice.

We did shoot a scene where Wonder Woman puts the lasso around me and we kind of tussle, but those scenes were cut.

Episode #34: "The Man Who Wouldn't Tell"
Airdate: March 31, 1978
Writer: Anne Collins
Director: Alan Crosland

Scientists working for Hopewell Industry have been unsuccessful in creating a new explosive material. When a night janitor accidentally completes the formula and causes an explosion, he goes on the run. After a competing company finds out what has happened, they hunt him down in order to attain this valuable information. Making her way into the rival company, Wonder Woman tracks the janitor down and uses her lasso to erase his memory of how he completed the formula to prevent it from falling into the wrong hands.

Lasso Tips

This is Eve's final episode.

WW Toys

Wonder Woman throws a man into a huge laundry washer and throws another man onto a pipe near the ceiling.

Wonder Woman bends a gun tip, pulls out elevator controls, and pulls the handles, wires, and steering wheel from a car.

Wonder Guest Stars
Gary Burghoff "Alan Akroy"
Burghoff is best known as Radar on the hit TV show "*M*A*S*H*. He was nominated for seven Emmys for that role and won in 1977 for Outstanding Continuing Performance by a Supporting Actor in a Comedy Series.

Episode #35: "The Girl from Islandia"
Airdate: April 7, 1978
Writer: Anne Collins
Director: Dick Moder

A newspaper publisher pulls an unconscious girl out of the water and asks Diana to help find out who she is. Wonder Woman uses her powers to awaken the young girl. As Diana befriends her, they learn that her name is Amadonna; she is from another dimension and possesses superpowers. After she is kidnapped, Amadonna's capturer wants to brainwash her in order to use her powers for evil.

Lasso Tips

This episode is rumored to be a proposed spin-off of a new TV series based on Amadonna's character.

WW Toys

Wonder Woman asks Tiger the dog to find her if Amadonna is kidnapped.

Wonder Woman uses her lasso to erase the memories of the men who know Amadonna's real identity.

Wonder Woman bends metal bars and breaks out of the glass tube.

Wonder Woman uses her tiara as a shape of a boomerang.

Wonder Guest Star
Tiger the Dog "Tiger"
Tiger is best known for his role as the family dog Tiger in the hit TV series *The Brady Bunch*.

Episode #36: "The Murderous Missile"
Airdate: April 21, 1978
Writer: Dick Nelson
Director: Dick Moder

A helmet that uses human brain waves to direct missiles has been created. As Diana is on her way to a missile countdown using this new technology, she is forced off the road and gets stuck in a small, desolate town that doesn't have any phone access. While there, Diana uncovers that the entire town is filled with imposters setting up a base camp to steal the new helmet in order to hold the world for ransom.

Lasso Tips

Diana drives a blue convertible Mercedes Benz with
    license plate 595TYY.
The missile is named Athena, who was a Greek goddess.

WW Toys

Wonder Woman breaks the chains holding her and
    proceeds to break out of a cell. She also stops a car
    with her foot.
Wonder Woman sports her full-body aqua outfit, acces-
    sorized with a gold helmet to turn it into a biker outfit..

Season 3
The New Adventures of Wonder Woman
Network: CBS-TV
Years: 1978–1979

Episode #37: "My Teenage Idol Is Missing"
Airdate: September 22, 1978
Writer: Anne Collins
Director: Seymour Robbie

Teen idol star Lane Kincaid is in Los Angeles for his sold-out show when his number one fan, Whitney Springfield, sees Lane being kidnapped. Nobody believes her, since Lane is replaced by his long-lost twin brother, Michael. The man behind the kidnapping is asking Lane's manager for two million dollars for his return. Diana begins to believe Whitney's story. When Lane's brother does well on stage, the kidnappers have no leverage and plan to kill him.

Lasso Tips

Suzanne Crough, who played Tracy Partridge in the hit TV series *The Partridge Family*, is seen as one of the screaming girls in the opening of the episode.

Dawn Lyn, who played Whitney Springfield, is the real-life sister of Leif Garrett.

Lyle Waggoner's role is limited to two minutes and he only speaks to Diana over the phone.

WW Toys

Wonder Woman bends a gun.
Wonder Woman uses her lasso to scale the side of a hotel.
Wonder Woman is sporting her cape.
Wonder Woman sports her full-body aqua outfit, accessorized with a gold helmet to turn it into a biker outfit.

Wonder Guest Star

Leif Garrett "Lane Kincaid/Michael Kincaid"
Garrett was a teen idol in the seventies who had five albums from 1977 to 1981. In 1979 he had his own TV

special, "Leif Garrett Special," and roles in *Sgt. Pepper's Lonely Hearts Club Band, The Outsiders,* and most recently in *Dickie Roberts: Former Child Star.* Garrett sings two of his songs, "I Was Made for Dancing" (top-twenty hit) and "When I Think of You," from his 1978 LP *Feel the Need.*

Episode #38: "Hot Wheels"

Airdate: September 29, 1978
Writer: Dennis Landa
Director: Dick Moder

Diana arrives at a shipyard to pick up a Rolls-Royce that contains missile plans. When the crate is found empty, Diana realizes the car has been loaded into a truck. Wonder Woman spins into action to follow the truck, while Inspector Tim Bolt, who has been tracking the Rolls-Royce, begins a high-speed car chase. After an unsuccessful chase, Tim and Diana join forces as car competitors to bust the car ring and retrieve the missile plans.

Lasso Tips

Spy games ensue as they introduce a microphone brooch, a pen with a tape recorder, and a belt buckle with a camera.

WW Toys

Wonder Woman makes a high jump and throws an inner tube around escaping criminals.
Wonder Woman uses her lasso to erase the bad guy's memory.

Episode #39: "The Deadly Sting"

Airdate: October 6, 1978
Writer: Dick Nelson
Director: Alan Crosland

Professor Brubaker has developed a biodegradable dart that can temporarily control the motor functions of athletes, enabling him to place bets and make money to further his research. When the mob realizes the professor is behind this, they put the pressure on him to try to collect a ten-million-dollar bet. Wonder Woman comes to the rescue in time and the football game is replayed.

Lasso Tips

IRA makes a joke about wanting a corn beef on rye, hold the mayo.

Diana drives a powder-blue Mercedes two-door car with the license plate 7T6493.

Ron Ely plays Bill Michaels and answers his door without his shirt on. No wonder he played TV's Tarzan from 1966 to 1968.

WW Toys

Wonder Woman uses her bracelets to fend off gunfire.
Wonder Woman jumps through a glass window and jumps down the side of a building.

Wonder Guest Stars

Craig T. Nelson "Sam"
Nelson is best known for his work in the TV shows *My Name Is Earl*, *The District*, and *Coach*, for which he

GUEST STAR MEMORY: HARVEY JASON "PROFESSOR BRUBAKER"

"I loved doing *Wonder Woman* because I was crazy about Lynda Carter. She was so nice and I just loved her."

won an Emmy for Outstanding Lead Actor in a Comedy Series in 1989.

Los Angeles Rams
Players Lawrence McCutcheon, Roman Gabriel, and Deacon Jones guest star in this episode.

Episode #40: "The Fine Art of Crime"
Airdate: October 13, 1978
Writer: Anne Collins
Director: Dick Moder

Harold Farnum invites Diana to an art opening of lifelike statues by sculptor Henry Roberts. Determined to find out how Roberts creates the statues, Harold unwittingly is placed into suspended animation and becomes the newest statue. Roberts is able to control their animation and bring them back to mobility to steal valuable treasures. When Wonder Woman gets too close, he decides to make her a statue as well. With a sleight of hand, Wonder Woman outsmarts him.

Lasso Tips

This is the first episode in which we don't see Wonder
Woman do a new spin, except for two reused spins
from "The Feminum Mystique, Part 2" (episode 6)
and "Judgment from Outer Space, Part 2" (episode
11).

IRA the computer watches the TV series *Kojak*.

Rover plays a joke on Harold and leads him to the
broom closet and laughs.

The opening theme music now has a faster tempo.

In the unveiling of the Wonder Woman statue, her hair
is in front, and in the far shot her hair is behind her
shoulders on the right side.

WW Toys

Wonder Woman uses her lasso to stop a car in its
tracks.

Wonder Woman jumps into a room from a skylight in
the roof.

Wonder Guest Stars

Roddy McDowall "Henry Roberts"

This is McDowall's second appearance in the show. He
guest starred in "The Man Who Made Volcanoes" (episode 23).

Gavin MacLeod "Mr. Ellsworth"

MacLeod went on to play Captain Merrill Stubing in
The Love Boat for ten years. *The Love Boat* was produced by Douglas S. Cramer and Aaron Spelling.

Ed Begley Jr. "Harold Farnum"

Begley Jr. returns as character Harold Farnum, the fumbling son of Senator Farnum. His first episode was "Diana's Disappearing Act" (episode 29).

Episode #41: "Disco Devil"

Airdate: October 20, 1978

Writer: Alan Brennert

Director: Leslie H. Martinson

When a government official visits a local disco, he turns up with selective amnesia. The thoughts missing from his mind relate to top-secret information. Diana enlists telepath Del Franklin to assist her. Del learns that Nick Carbone, another telepath, is the one responsible for stealing this valuable information. Nick works out of the disco, which is a front for a black market information broker. The disco owner, Angelique, sends Nick to retrieve Del, not knowing that she plans to have Nick killed and have Del replace him. Diana investigates the disco, and as Wonder Woman, frees Del, who then uses his powers on Nick, which cancels out their abilities as telepaths.

Lasso Tips

Diana has a new apartment.

WW Toys

Wonder Woman lifts a car to keep it from moving, breaks down a door, and bends a chair.

Wonder Woman uses her bracelets to deflect bullets and as a glass cutter to cut her way out of a mirrored room.

Wonder Woman uses her tiara to knock a gun out of a man's hand.

Wonder Guest Stars
Wolfman Jack "DJ"
Wolfman Jack was a well-known DJ and personality in the seventies.

Russell Johnson "Corule"
Johnson is best known for his character the Professor in the classic TV series *Gilligan's Island*.

Episode #42: "Formicida"
Airdate: November 3, 1978
Writer: Katharyn Michaelian Powers
Director: Alan Crossland

Several buildings belonging to Harcourt Industries have been destroyed. Steve and Diana investigate. On her way to meet with a scientist, Wonder Woman encounters Formicida, a genetically altered woman with the strength of ants and who has the ability to communicate with them. Formicida is dead set on stopping Harcourt Industries from marketing the EF-11 pesticide, which is toxic when mixed with water and airborne sulfates. Wonder Woman, with the help of Rover, stops Formicida before she destroys another building that houses the pesticide.

Lasso Tips

This is the second episode in which we don't see
  Wonder Woman do her spin.
Wonder Woman jumps over the fence while holding
  Rover, but her hands are up when she is in the air.

WW Toys

Wonder Woman uses her lasso to have Dr. Irene Janis
  forget how she created the formula to turn into
  Formicida.

Wonder Guest Stars
Robert Shields "Dr. Doug Radcliff" and Lorene Yarnell
"Dr. Irene Janis/Formicida"
Shields and Yarnell were best known as the mime act
from *The Sonny and Cher Show*. They went on to have
their own self-titled TV series, *Shields and Yarnell*.

Episode #43: "Time Bomb"
Airdate: November 10, 1978
Writers: David Wise and Kathleen Barnes
Director: Seymour Robbie

In the year 2155, Adam Clement has made a time
portal. His greedy assistant Cassandra Loren decides to
use it to travel back to 1978 to make a fortune. She uses
her knowledge of the past to find the new energy source
Cabrium-90. Wonder Woman, with the help of Adam,
locates Cassandra and prevents the energy source from
being discovered.

Lasso Tips

Wonder Woman will still be alive in 2155.

Diana and Adam have a mutual attraction for each
   other. Maybe they'll meet up in the future?

Diana has a different apartment, which is seen only
   once more in "Skateboard Wizard" (episode 44).

The Griffith Observatory doubles as Washington, D.C.'s
   Winchester Observatory.

Downtown Los Angeles can be seen in the shots from
   the observatory.

Century City Mall doubles as the Westside Plaza Mall.

WW Toys

Wonder Woman bends a gun around a hit man's neck.

Wonder Woman uses her lasso to pull Cassandra off her
   horse.

Wonder Guest Stars

Joan Van Ark "Cassandra Loren" / Ted Shackelford
"Adam Clement"

This dynamic duo are best known for their roles in
both *Dallas* and *Knots Landing* as Val and Gary Ewing.
This was the first time the twosome worked together.

Episode #44: "Skateboard Wiz"

Airdate: November 24, 1978

Writer: Alan Brennert

Director: Leslie H. Martinson

   Diana is going on vacation to San Corona, California,
to visit friends, Leslie and Jamie O'Neil. A ruthless busi-
nessman, Evan Donalsen, wants to turn the quiet city of

Corona Beach into the new Las Vegas. He already runs a hidden casino and his next move is to create a convention center. His arson tactics force people of the city to get out of his way. Jamie stumbles onto Donalsen's plans at the casino and becomes a target for death.

Lasso Tip

Diana loves anchovies on pizza.

This is the episode that fans call "The Blow Drier Spin" in which Wonder Woman comes out of the water, spins, and her hair is dry.

Wonder Woman jumps into the burning building—watch the smoke because it also goes the opposite way back into the building.

The Santa Monica Pier is used, as well as the Santa Corona Beach Club.

This is the last time Diana's new apartment is seen.

Farrah Fawcett is mentioned in this episode!

WW Toys

Wonder Woman's lasso is used to get information.

Wonder Woman uses her superstrength to throw a surfboard to stop a man, breaks a chair and smashes a bullet holder, breaks two holes in a door, and bends a towel rack to hold a thug into place.

Flying Fashions

Wonder Woman spins into her skateboard outfit, which is her basic WW outfit with a red helmet with a gold star on the front and red gloves with red-and-white arm and knee pads.

Wonder Guest Stars

Eric Braeden "Donalsen"

Braeden returns for his second guest appearance. He was in the pilot episode as the Nazi pilot. Braeden is best known for his role as Victor Newman on the soap opera *The Young and the Restless*.

Episode #45: "The Deadly Dolphin"

Airdate: December 1, 1978

Writer: Jackson Gillis

Director: Sigmund Neufeld Jr.

Dr. Sylvia Stubbs and a dolphin named Bluebeard are kidnapped. It's discovered that Bluebeard is a Navy research dolphin. His service records have been stolen and it's unknown what he is trained for. Mr. Lockland uses Bluebeard to set explosive missiles on a large oil tanker in order to create an oil spill so he can monopolize the coastal property.

WW Toys

Wonder Woman uses her superstrength to bend a shotgun; kicks a door in with her foot and throws a man up to the ceiling beams; throws the bomb away; jumps to the top of a building; and breaks through a glass ceiling.

Wonder Woman clicks her bracelets together to scare the sharks away.

Flying Fashions

The second time she turns into the aqua suit she does
not have her fins, but she has them in the water. Fans
call this one the "submariner outfit."

Episode #46: "Stolen Faces"

Airdate: December 15, 1978
Writers: Richard Carr and Anne Collins
Director: Leslie H. Martinson

The IADC is notified when a woman dressed as
Wonder Woman is brought into the hospital unconscious. Diana learns that fashion designer Edgar Percy
plans to use people with criminal records to imperson-
ate Wonder Woman, Steve Trevor, and other agents of
the IADC to help steal millions of dollars in jewels from
wealthy guests who plan to attend a big fashion show.

Lasso Tips

Wonder Woman only says two words in the entire
episode: "Hold it."
Diana falls from a parking garage and spins in midair
into Wonder Woman.
The Los Angeles Airport Marriott doubles as the Myer-
ton Hotel and was also used in "Knockout" (episode
19) and "Spaced Out" (episode 50).

WW Toys

Wonder Woman uses her superstrength as Diana
Prince.

Wonder Guest Stars

Bob Seagren "Roman"

Seagren won Olympic gold in 1968 for the pole vault. This is Seagren's first appearance on Wonder Woman. He was set to be in a spin-off show. The show's pilot episode was "The Man Who Could Not Die" (episode 58).

Jeannie Epper "Second Wonder Woman imposter"

Epper was one of Lynda Carter's stunt doubles on the series.

Episode #47: "Pot of Gold" (The Holiday Episode)

Airdate: December 22, 1978

Writer: Michael McGreevey

Director: Gordon Hessler

Diana is in England tracking Trackery, the man who has created perfect reproduction plates of the U.S. one-hundred-dollar bills. Stateside, Bonelli is searching for gold to buy the counterfeit plates and steals leprechaun Patrick O'Hanlon's pot of gold to finish off the transaction. Patrick follows his gold, but it's Trackery who has been double-crossed by Bonelli.

Lasso Tip

Steve is out of the office and back in the field helping
    Diana on this case.

Patrick O'Hanlon the leprechaun knows Wonder
    Woman's true identity.

Christmas music plays during the opening scenes.

WW Toys

Wonder Woman uses her superstrength to jump on an airplane then jump to the top of a building. She pushes a large metal garbage bin and rides standing upright on the truck. She also catches the leprechaun falling from the helicopter, throws sixty-pound weights, and catches a large box.

Wonder Woman's lasso is used to try to get information and pulls down a helicopter.

Wonder Woman uses her bracelets to deflect gunshots.

Episode #48: "Gault's Brain"

Airdate: December 29, 1978
Teleplay: Arthur Weingarten
Story: John Gaynor
Director: Gordon Hessler

Harlow Gult, the owner of Gult Industries, has recently died. Yet, Gult is alive; at least his brain is and is able to communicate through psychokinesis. He is seeking a younger, sexier body to take over and Olympic hopeful, Morton Danzig, fits the bill quite nicely. Wonder Woman uncovers the evil plan of killing Danzig and must save Danzig.

Lasso Tips

Steve has a picture of his father, Major Steve Trevor, on his desk.

This is the second episode that shows a dead body. The first one is "Anschluss 77" (episode 16).

WW Toys

Wonder Woman's lasso is used find out the truth.
Wonder Woman uses her superstrength to throw bullets without the shotgun and hits three targets at a time.
Wonder Woman's tiara is used to stop the machine that was going to cut open a man's head.

Flying Fashions!

Wonder Woman spins into her aqua suit while trapped in a barrel at the bottom of the lake.

Shirtless Hunk Alert

David Mason Daniels plays the sexy hunk Morton. He went on to play Jerry Baldwin on *Days of Our Lives*.

Episode #49: "Going, Going, Gone"
Airdate: January 12, 1979
Teleplay: Anne Collins and Patrick Mathews
Story: Patrick Mathews
Director: Alan Crosland

A Soviet jet fighter pilot is tricked into thinking he is crashing into a UFO and drops his nuclear warhead into the ocean, where it's retrieved to be sold to the highest bidder. Diana takes on the cover of mercenary Mrs. Fox, and joins the bidding war for the nuclear warhead. Sheldon Como, a double agent, blows Diana's cover. To eliminate Diana, they shoot her out of a torpedo tube. She transforms into Wonder Woman and sinks the whole deal.

WW Toys

Wonder Woman uses her superstrength to stop a box
   falling and bends steel beams.
Wonder Woman's bracelets are used to deflect beam
   rays and bullets.

Flying Fashions!

Wonder Woman changes into her aqua outfit as she is
   jettisoned out of a torpedo tube.

Episode #50: "Spaced Out"

Airdate: January 26, 1979
Writer: Bill Taylor
Director: Ivan Dixon

   Kimball, a thief, breaks into the observatory to steal
the collimating crystals, which have the power to create a deadly laser. Diana comes to Los Angeles to retrieve the stolen crystals and checks into a hotel where
a science fiction convention is being held. Kimball discovers that the crystals have been sent to the convention
by mistake and takes the place of the Black Avenger as
a cover.

Lasso Tips

Something unknown is seen flying out of Wonder
   Woman's hair during one of her spins.
Robby the Robot from *Lost in Space* has a guest appear-
   ance.

Griffith Observatory in Los Angeles doubles in this
    episode as the Torrance Observatory.
The outside shot of the hotel is once again the Los
    Angeles Airport Marriott.

WW Toys

Wonder Woman uses her superstrength to catch a huge
    falling plant.
Wonder Woman uses her lasso to rescue the man that
    Diana pushed into the pool.

Shirtless Hunk Alert

The man behind the Black Avenger is seen tied up and
    gagged only in his underwear. The role was played by
    Ken Wilson.

Wonder Guest Stars

Rene Auberjonois "Kimball"
Auberjonois is best known for his work in *Benson, Star
Trek: Deep Space Nine,* and most recently, *Boston Legal.*

Episode #51: "The Starships Are Coming"

Airdate: February 2, 1979
Teleplay: Glen Olson, Rod Baker, and Anne Collins
Story: Glen Olson and Rod Baker
Director: Alan Crossland

A town is overtaken by a fleet of UFO starships,
which is being telecast live on TV. Colonel Robert El-
liot, an alien expert, believes that the invasion is true.
The aliens make contact with the colonel and tell him

they want to wipe out our planet to steal our natural resources. The aliens instruct him to launch nuclear warheads toward China. Wonder Woman goes on TV to stop the launch and to explain that the attacks were all a hoax.

Lasso Tips

Bobbie is Steve's new secretary and is only seen in this episode.

WW Toys

Wonder Woman uses her superstrength to pull her car out of a ditch, and to flip a car so that the bad guys can't get away.
Wonder Woman's bracelets are used to fend off bullets.
Wonder Woman's lasso is used to find out the whole scheme.

Wonder Guest Stars
Sheryl Lee Ralph "Bobbie"
Ralph is best known for her work in TV's *Designing Women* as Etienne Toussaint Bouvier and had recurring roles on *Moesha, The District,* and *Barbershop.* She won an Independent Spirit Award for Best Supporting Female in the film *To Sleep with Anger* in 1990.

David White "General"
White is best known for his role as Larry Tate in *Bewitched* and was in the film *The Apartment,* which won the Oscar for Best Picture in 1960.

Episode #52: "Amazon Hot Wax"

Airdate: February 16, 1979
Writer: Alan Brennert
Director: Ryan Austin

In Hollywood, the disappearance of singing sensation Billy Dero has shaken the record industry. Diana goes undercover as Kathy Meadows, Phoenix Record's newest young singing starlet, to find out about Dero's disappearance. She uncovers that record producer, Eric Landau, is being blackmailed for Dero's final recording for one million dollars. When the music group, Antimatter, finds Dero alive, Eric stops paying the blackmail money and Dero becomes a real target for death.

Lasso Tips

Lynda sings two songs in this episode: "Want to Get Beside You" and "Toto." They were included on her LP *Portrait,* which was released in 1979 on Epic Records.

This episode was tied up in legal issues in the 1990s due to the music releases for Lynda Carter's songs themselves. It was later resolved for the release onto DVD through Warner Brothers.

A poster of John Travolta is mentioned.

Elton John's Hollywood Walk of Fame star is seen.

WW Toys

Wonder Woman uses superstrength to jump out of a window and fly.

Wonder Woman's lasso is used on a thug to find out information.

Wonder Guest Stars

Sarah Purcell "Barbi Gordon"

Purcell was best known as one of the cohosts of the TV show *Real People*.

Judge Reinhold "Jeff Gordon"

This was Reinhold's first TV appearance. He later had a very successful movie career with *Fast Times at Ridgemont High*, *Stripes*, *Beverly Hills Cop*, and *The Santa Claus*.

Rick Springfield "Anton"

This is Springfield's second appearance in *Wonder Woman*. He was also seen in "Screaming Javelins" (episode 28). Springfield won a Grammy for his song "Jessie's Girl" and played Dr. Noah Drake on *General Hospital*.

Episode #53: "The Richest Man in the World"

Airdate: February 19, 1979

Writer: Jackson Gillis and Ann Collins

Director: Don MacDougall

Marshall Henshaw, the richest man in the world, makes an appearance at a political cocktail party for the prime minster who is buying "Missy," his Missile Systems Scrambler, which can scramble the guidance of any missile five hundred miles away. Diana proves the authenticity of Missy, but Missy is replaced with a fake to be sold on the black market.

Lasso Tips

The dog dish is full and then it's not.
Diana's purse breaks when she gets held up and later it's fixed.

WW Toys

Wonder Woman's lasso is used to save a truck and get information.
Wonder Woman uses her superstrength to throw sticks of dynamite and jump onto high beams in a garage.

Wonder Guest Stars
Barry Miller "Barney"
Miller is best known for his role as Bobby C. in the film *Saturday Night Fever* and Ralph in TV's *Fame*.

Episode #54: "A Date with Doomsday"
Airdate: March 10, 1979
Writer: Roland Starke and Dennis Landa
Director: Curtis Harrington

A warfare virus has been stolen; if it becomes airborne it will destroy red blood cells and cause death. If an antibody is not found, no living creature is safe. Professor Zander discovers an antidote, but as soon as the new antidote has been created, it's stolen. The plan is to release the first dose of the deadly virus on the steps of the White House.

Lasso Tips

Wonder Woman's name is never mentioned in this
    episode, except for the opening credits.
The character name Kurt Baker is an inside joke. The
    real Kurt Baker worked on the series.

WW Toys

Wonder Woman uses her superstrength to jump over a
    truck.
Wonder Woman's lasso is used to save George when he
    jumps off the roof.
Wonder Woman uses her mind powers to speak to
    doves for a tip.

Flying Fashions

Wonder Woman spins into her motorbike outfit.

Wonder Guest Stars

Donnelly Rhodes "Ward Selkirk"
Rhodes is best known for his current role as Dr. Cottle
in the Sci Fi Channel's *Battlestar Galactica (2004)*.

Hermione Baddeley "Mrs. Mary Jane Tripp"
Baddeley was nominated for an Oscar for Best Actress
in a Supporting Role in *Room at the Top* (1959) and won
a Golden Globe in 1976 for her work as Mrs. Nell Naug-
atuck in *Maude*. She is most recognized for her work in
Mary Poppins.

Episode #55: "The Girl with a Gift for Disaster"

Airdate: March 17, 1979
Writer: Alen Brennert
Director: Alan Crosland

Bonnie Murphy, the girlfriend of small-time thief Mark Reuben, seems to be jinxed, but really she has untapped telekinetic powers. Reuben's next job is to steal J. R. Electronics' microwave scrambler, which can jam signals across bandwidths and could stop all phone, TV, and radio communications. Bonnie unknowingly creates an accident that allows Mark to steal the microwave scrambler.

Lasso Tips

This is actress Jane Actman's (Bonnie Murphy) second appearance on the series; she was also seen in "The Man Who Wouldn't Tell" (episode 34).

WW Toys

Wonder Woman's bracelets are used to deflect gunfire.
Wonder Woman's lasso is used to find out information and erase memories.
Wonder Woman uses her superstrength to break a boulder with her own hands, bend a gun, and break a sword in half.

Episode #56: "The Boy Who Knew Her Secret, Part 1"

Airdate: May 28, 1979
Writer: Anne Collins
Director: Leslie H. Martinson

Dr. Jaffe has Diana go to Crystal Lake, California, to investigate a meteor shower. The shower is a group of mirrored tetrahedrons that trap human souls so aliens can take over their bodies. The aliens have come to Earth to capture a murderer from their planet. Steven "Skip" Keller is the first to realize that his friends and family are acting odd. Skip partners up with Diana to find out what is happening. When the group wants to turn Skip into an alien, Diana turns into Wonder Woman, not realizing that Skip sees the transformation.

Lasso Tips

A year later, in 1980, the name "Crystal Lake" became infamous in the horror classic film series *Friday the 13th*.

WW Toys

Wonder Woman's bracelets are used to defend herself from gunfire.

Wonder Guest Star

Clark Brandon "Skip Keller"
Brandon was an eighties teen heartthrob. He starred in the eighties TV series *Mr. Merlin* as Zachary Rogers.

Episode #57: "The Boy Who Knew Her Secret, Part 2"

Airdate: May 29, 1979
Writer: Anne Collins
Director: Leslie H. Martinson

The creature the aliens are after can turn into any form and currently has chosen Cameron Michael. After Cameron sees Diana turn into Wonder Woman he uses his powers to have her forget she is Wonder Woman. The aliens need the final piece of the tetrahedron to entrap Michael, which Skip has. Michael transforms into Wonder Woman to retrieve the final piece; however Skip sees through the trick, knowing Diana is really Wonder Woman. Skip helps Diana remember that she is Wonder Woman so she can battle and capture Michael. After the aliens leave, Wonder Woman uses her lasso to erase Skip's memory of her secret. Later, Skip listens to an audio tape on which he has told himself that Diana Prince is really Wonder Woman.

WW Toys

Wonder Woman's lasso is used to find out why the aliens are on Earth and to erase Skip's memory of who Diana really is.

Wonder Woman uses her superstrength to run superfast and defeat the alien.

Episode #58: "The Man Who Could Not Die"

Airdate: August 28, 1979
Writer: Anne Collins
Director: John Newland

Diana is moving into her new Los Angeles home. During the move, a chimpanzee is struck by a truck and is mysteriously unharmed. Joseph Reichman, a radiation molecular biologist who has made the invincible chimpanzee, now wants to create an invincible man by injecting athlete Bryce Kandel with the serum. Reichman's dream is to create an army of invincible men to take over the world.

Lasso Tips

According to Bob Seagren, this episode was designed to be a spin-off show to star Bob Seagren as the invincible man.

This episode was to be the final episode of season three and was aired out of sequence.

Lyle Waggoner has been taken out of the opening sequence, and new show clips were included..

Diana's new home address: 409 S. Vine, Los Angeles, CA.

WW Toys

Wonder Woman uses her superstrength to move a very large safe.

Flying Fashions

Wonder Woman is seen wearing her cape.

Wonder Guest Stars/New Cast

Bob Seagren "Bryce Kandel"

This is his second appearance on the series; he was also in "Stolen Faces" (episode 46). Seagren won Olympic gold in 1968 for the pole vault.

John Durren was to play Dale Hawthorn from the IADC.

James Bond III was to play the young kid T. Burton Phipps III.

Episode #59: "The Phantom of the Roller Coaster, Part 1"

Airdate: September 4, 1979
Writer: Anne Collins
Director: John Newland

Mobster Harrison Fynch wants to buy an amusement park from Leon Gurney to set up shop in Washington, D.C. Leon will not sell to Fynch, who then has a bomb placed on the Crazy Wheel to force his hand. As a goon plants the bomb, Dave Gurney, Leon's disfigured brother who lives below the park, disarms the bomb. Wonder Woman tries to catch Dave, but he disappears into the tunnels under the park.

Lasso Tips

The Watergate Hotel is where Harrison Fynch is to be staying while in D.C. It's the complex where the 1972 Watergate scandal occurred.

The Fun Universe Amusement Park was filmed at the Warner Brothers–owned theme park, Six Flags, in Valencia, California.

WW Toys

Wonder Woman uses her superstrength to kick a car off the road, and jumps up and down on the roller coaster.
Wonder Woman once again uses her lasso to find out information.

Flying Fashions

Wonder Woman spins into her motorcycle outfit—the blue bodysuit with helmet and gloves. The helmet has two red stars and one white with three stripes.

Wonder Guest Stars

Ike Eisenmann "Randy"
Ike is best known for the Walt Disney's films *Return from Witch Mountain* and *Escape to Witch Mountain*. He also costared in the seventies sci-fi show *The Fantastic Journey* and played Midshipman Peter Preston in *Star Trek: The Wrath of Khan*.

Episode #60: "The Phantom of the Roller Coaster, Part 2"

Airdate: September 11, 1979
Writer: Anne Collins
Director: John Newland

As Fynch is preparing to make his move to buy the park, Steve and Diana decide to set a trap and arrest him with Leon's help. After Fynch is arrested, Wonder Woman convinces Dave that he should come up from beneath the park and face his fears and reconnect with his loved ones.

Lasso Tips

Wonder Woman just shows up without a spin after Diana's car is run off the road. This is the final episode of the series.

WW Toys

Wonder Woman uses her superstrength to hold up a roller coaster.

Wonder Woman runs across D.C. to capture Fynch and does a double flip off a tall building.

Wonder Woman's lasso is used to find out information and makes Randy forget where he has been all week.

CLOSE-UP

Lasso of Truth with Dick Van Patten, Episode #4: "Beauty on Parade"

How was it working on Wonder Woman*?*
I played a magician. I thought they would just have me do some trick stuff. Instead, they sent me to this school for magicians. They had a famous magician work with me. He taught me how to do the trick. I put Wonder Woman in the cabinet and I turned the cabinet around and she disappeared. They actually had me do the trick on TV. It was fun.

How was it working with Lynda?
Very nice. She was wonderful and Lyle Waggoner and I became very good friends through that show.

Lasso of Truth with Vincent Van Patten, Episodes #24 & 25: "Mind Stealers from Outer Space Parts 1 & 2"

How was it filming your episode of Wonder Woman*?*
It was a two-part episode and I think we shot it at the Los Angeles Zoo. It was summertime and very hot in the valley. I played an alien. It was kind of easy. I fell into the part, very robotic, and it was a lot of fun. It was one of those jobs that you take the money and run.

How was it working with Lynda Carter?
On the set, it struck me while she was wearing the outfit how beautiful she was and how gigantic she was. She was truly Wonder Woman; beautifully proportioned and a very tall girl. You could not take your eyes off of her eyes. She had absolutely the most beautiful blue eyes that were striking. She was very nice.

How was it doing the alien screeching?
That's right! We did a type of screeching. The director told us to do some type of mouthing off and they would put the screeching in later. It was strange. Here is Wonder Woman and we're supposed to be aliens and we

didn't have any costumes or anything. We were supposed to look very normal.

What did you think about the Zardor?
It was looking like something out of Power Rangers. It
was pretty tacky, I believe!

Were you a fan of Wonder Woman?
I wasn't really a comic book reader. It was just one of
those shows which caught on with people. Kind of
looked to me like an updated version of the Batman series with a beautiful woman.

Lasso of Truth
with
Joan Van Ark,
Episode #43: "Time Bomb"

How was it playing a bad girl?
Oh, how wonderful! I think her name was "Cassandra." Donna [Mills] has always told me those are the funnest parts! We did the *Today Show* recently and they said, "Poor Valene," and I said, "No, No, the poorer the better!" When there is more drama, more against the grain, it's way more fun. Cassandra was fun to play.

The funny irony is that I worked with Ted [Shackelford]. The original Gary Ewing was David Ackroyd, who was doing a TV movie at Universal and he couldn't get out of it. He was the male lead in the film *Little Women* and *Knots Landing* was going to pilot and they were pretty sure they were going to series with it being a spin-off of *Dallas*. The producers called me to say who they were looking at to play my husband [Gary]. They said that they were pretty high on a guy named Ted Shackelford and we understand you just worked with him. I said, 'No way. We're too much alike. We're both high strung and we would never be compatible. Forget it.' And at the table read who am I sitting across from . . . Ted Shackelford, who of course was flawless as Gary [Ewing].

From my *Knots Landing* years, there are three

costars that are a part of my DNA now—Michele [Lee], Ted [Shackelford], and Julie [Harris]. We are very, very close. I still love the fact that I said, 'No, don't even think about Ted Shackelford,' not ever knowing that we would work fifteen years together after *Wonder Woman*.

How was that "space age" computer set?
I remember two long days spent in sort of a cubbyhole set, which was sort of the main control center. It was a bit claustrophobic.

Your outfits where so "modern day" but how about Ted Shackelford's outfit?
Ted was always dressed like a giant condom [laughing]. The costume he had on was just insane. Someone surprised me with a clip from it on an interview show and sure enough he did look like a giant condom! I think that's why they got the clip, to prove I'm not nuts. That's what he looked like. [laughing]

You were also a superhero yourself . . . the voice of Spider-Woman!
Oh yes! *Spider-Woman*, the ABC animated show, yes! [laughing] I was doing that while on *Knots Landing*. I had to do two different voices. One that was the normal Jessica Drew, and the one that was Spider-Woman, balls to the wall, who could conquer and take care of anything. It was a fun job!

Now my daughter Vanessa [Marshall] is working on a Sony Studios cartoon *The Spectacular Spider-Man Animated Series*. She is doing the part of Mary Jane

Watson and it has already been picked up for the second season.

The Spider-Woman twirl is just like Lynda's Wonder Woman spin.
Yes, you're right. It is like Lynda's. They may have patterned it after that. I don't know for sure. That's interesting. I didn't realize that parallel.

How was it working with Lynda?
I adore her. Killer gorgeous! She still is and always will be . . . and she has a body to die for.

Lasso of Truth with Bob Seagren, Episode #58: "The Man Who Could Not Die"

How was it working with Lynda?

She was great. We were personal friends with her and her husband at the time, Ron Samuels. I used to own a travel agency. I started doing their travel and that is how we met. Through mutual friends we would see each other at dinner parties too.

I eventually went in and read for an episode and got the part. It was a small part. Then they came back and it was for "The Man Who Couldn't Die." It was slated to be a spin-off series like *Wonder Woman*. A "Wonder Man" to some degree, about a guy who has various powers. That's what they filmed it as. There was a very extensive search for the lead and I felt pretty happy to get it. Then it never went any farther than an episode of *Wonder Woman*. This was one of my seven pilots that never got picked up for series [laughs]. No wonder I got out of the business.

Was Wonder Woman to be a part of this new series?

They explained to me that it was going to be a spin-off series. I don't know what the relationship would have been with Wonder Woman. I don't think they intended to call it Wonder Man, but I don't know for sure.

How was it working on the set?
It was fun. Lynda was a very nice, easygoing person. My wife and I were personal friends with Lyle and Sharon Waggoner. It was fun working with them because we knew each other and we did some things socially. It was pretty painless and it was nice to do the show.

How about all your stunts?
I remember they did everything to me they could in that one show. They set me on fire, electrocuted me, and had a lion attack me. They blew me up and threw me out a window and I remember they put this stuff that smokes on clothing. They told me to put on some kind of undersuit to protect your skin and apparently that got overlooked. I had something on but it wasn't the right material and they started brushing all this stuff on my back. When I hit the ground it looked like I was smoking or smoldering. I remember lying there on the ground and it was like "god this stuff is burning, this is getting hot." Pretty soon I was up and I couldn't get out of those clothes fast enough. Everybody was saying "Oh my God, where's his suit"—the one I was supposed to have on. I remember going down to some clinic there swabbing my back; that stuff put some blisters on my skin, but nothing too bad.

Then they had this great big lion on the set; of course everyone just scattered. They had a stunt double lying on the floor wrestling with this thing. I'm so glad I didn't have to do that.

"Lynda Carter as Wonder Woman" by artist Glen Hanson
(© glenhanson.com) (© CBS/Warner Brothers)

CHAPTER SEVEN

TV's Wonder Woman Collectibles

HERE IS a quick guide to begin collecting items that were made for the seventies' *Wonder Woman* TV series! When the series was released many toys were produced, but many without mention of the TV series or with Lynda Carter's image on them.

Kyall Coulton shared his Wonder Woman toy knowledge to compile this list. Check out Coulton's webstie www.wonderwomancollectors.com for everything collectible on Wonder Woman!

Item: Wonder Woman Cathy Lee Crosby Promo Poster
Manufacturer/Year: ABC/1974
Description: 25" x 32". Text reads, "Cathy Lee Crosby as
    Wonder Woman an ABC Movie of the Week."

Item: Lynda Carter Wonder Woman Alarm Clock
Manufacturer/Year: Toastmaster Inc/Ingraham Time
    Products – 197?
Description: Featuring an image of Lynda Carter as
    Wonder Woman with red-and-yellow background.

Item: Wonder Woman "Lynda Carter" Doll

Manufacturer/Year: Mego/1976

Description: The eagle-crested red–and-yellow bodice
was painted onto the doll, while the removable
blue-and-white starred shorts were made of cloth. The
bracelets were made of silver plastic and were also
removable, as were the red knee-high boots and tiara.
The doll also came with a golden lasso, a Navy-style
Diana Prince uniform complete with high-heeled
shoes and glasses, and a display stand.

Facts: A mold of Lynda Carter's face was made to make
the doll look as similar to her as possible. Additional
character dolls were produced for Steve Trevor,
Queen Hippolyta, and Nubia. When the doll was
reissued, Lynda Carter's name and image were
removed from the packaging.

Item: Complete Visual Guidebook of Wonder Woman

Manufacturer/Year: Town Mook/1980/Produced in Japan

Description: Soft cover. 105 pages. Contains over 1,000
images along with a pullout double-sided poster. One
side features an image of Lynda as Wonder Woman,
the other side features animation cells from the
opening sequences of the show.

Item: Wonder Woman/Lynda Carter Jigsaw Puzzle

Manufacturer/Year: APC /1977

Description: 121 pieces. Features image of Wonder
Woman deflecting bullets and contains a small
picture of Lynda Carter in the center.

Item: Lynda Carter is Wonder Woman Jigsaw Puzzle
(version #1)

Manufacturer/Year: APC /1977

Description: 200 pieces. Features image of Lynda Carter
in full Wonder Woman costume (ABC era) including
cape.

Item: Lynda Carter is Wonder Woman Jigsaw Puzzle
(version #2)

Manufacturer/Year: APC /1977

Description: 551 pieces. Features image of Lynda Carter
(not in Wonder Woman costume).

Item: Lynda Carter is Wonder Woman Jigsaw Puzzle
(version #3)

Manufacturer/Year: APC /1978

Description: 200 pieces. Features image of Lynda Carter in
full Wonder Woman costume (CBS era) including cape.

Item: Lynda Carter is Wonder Woman Jigsaw Puzzle
(version #4)

Manufacturer/Year: APC /1978

Description: 200 pieces. Features image of Lynda Carter
in full Wonder Woman costume (CBS era) with
hands on hips.

Item: Wonder Woman Lynda Carter Mirror

Manufacturer/Year: Unknown

Description: Featuring images of Lynda Carter as
Wonder Woman wearing a combination of the ABC
and CBS versions of the costume.

Item: Lynda Carter Wonder Woman Phone Card Set

Manufacturer/Year: Patco/1997

Description: Set of four $10 cards that form a full picture
of Lynda Carter as Wonder Woman (CBS costume)
when put together. Cards are numbered Patco
Adventure/Fantasy Cards #23, #24, #25, and #26.

Item: Wonder Woman Lynda Carter Statue
Manufacturer/Year: Terry Reynolds/1997
Description: Approximately 15". Statue of Lynda Carter
as Wonder Woman (ABC costume), with gold lasso.

Item: Lynda Carter as Wonder Woman Statue
Manufacturer/Year: DC Direct/2007
Description: Approximately 13". Porcelain statue of
Lynda Carter as Wonder Woman wearing the cos-
tume from the CBS series. The statue can be removed
from the gold star base. Sculpted by Tim Bruckner.
Comes with Certificate of Authenticity.

Item: Wonder Woman Lynda Carter Promo Hand Fan
Manufacturer/Year: In2TV/2006
Description: Promotional cardboard die-cut fan in the
shape of Lynda Carter's head. Front features headshot
of Lynda as Wonder Woman. Back features an image
of Lynda as Wonder Woman lifting the back of a car
advertising the Wonder Woman television series,
which can be viewed at In2TV's Web site.

Item: Lynda Carter as Wonder Woman Poster (version #1)
Manufacturer/Year: Thought Factory/1977
Description: 23" x 35". Features full-body image of Lynda
Carter in full Wonder Woman costume (ABC era)
including cape and hands on hips. Gray background.

Item: Lynda Carter as Wonder Woman Poster
(version #2)
Manufacturer/Year: Thought Factory/1977
Description: 23" x 35". Features full-body image of Lynda
Carter in full Wonder Woman costume (CBS era) and
hands on hips. Red background with white stars.

Item: Wonder Woman Bus Shelter Poster
Manufacturer/Year: Retro TV/ 2004
Description: 55" x 39". Promotional poster from Argen-
tina advertising Wonder Woman's return to cable
television. Features image of Lynda as Wonder
Woman with hands on hips from the episode "The
Bermuda Triangle Crisis." Text in Spanish reads El
Deseo De Volver A Verla Estaba Dando Vueltas En
Tu Cabeza.

Item: Wonder Woman Season One DVD Promotional
Poster
Manufacturer/Year: Warner Bros/2004 /Produced in
Canada
Description: 27" x 39.5". Advertisement for the release of
Wonder Woman Season One DVD set.

Item: Lynda Carter Wonder Woman Promo Poster
Manufacturer/Year: Hallmark/2007
Description: 18" x 24". Cardboard advertisement of
Lynda Carter as Wonder Woman used in stores to
promote Hallmark's range of talking greeting cards.

Item: Wonder Woman The Collector's Edition VHS
Manufacturer/Year: Columbia House/2000

Description: Featuring episodes from the entire series
except "The Pied Piper," "Amazon Hot Wax," "My
Teenage Idol Is Missing," "Flight to Oblivion," and
"The Starships Are Coming." Each VHS tape contains
two episodes.

Item: The New Adventures of Wonder Woman
Vol. 1 & 2 DVD
Manufacturer/Year: Warner Home Video/2003/Produced
in England
Description: Volume 1 features episodes "The Return of
Wonder Woman," "Anschluss '77", and "The Man
Who Could Move the World." Special features in-
clude photo gallery, Wonder Woman memorabilia,
and cast profiles. Volume 2 features "The Bermuda
Triangle Crisis," "Knockout", and "The Queen and
the Thief." Special features include photo gallery,
Wonder Woman memorabilia, and History of Won-
der Woman (text).

Item: Wonder Woman The Complete Series DVD
Manufacturer/Year: Warner Home Video/2004–2005
Description:
    Season One. Three discs including pilot movie.
Special features include commentary by Lynda Carter
and Douglas Cramer on the pilot episode and docu-
mentary *Beauty, Brawn and Bulletproof Bracelets: A
Wonder Woman Retrospective*. Packaging contains
facts and trivia about Wonder Woman.
    Season Two. Four discs. Special features include
documentary *Revolutionizing a Classic: From Comic
Book to Television*.

Season Three. Four discs. Special features include audio commentary by Lynda Carter on episode "My Teenage Idol Is Missing," and documentary *Wonder Woman: The Ultimate Feminist Icon.*

Item: Original Soundtrack Theme from the ABC Series Wonder Woman LP

Manufacturer/Year: Shadybrook Records/1977

Description: 7" LP. Theme by New World Symphony. Cover features black-and-white artwork from the #165 comic book cover of Wonder Woman.

Item: Theme from the ABC Series Wonder Woman LP "Tema De La Mujer Maravilla"

Manufacturer/Year: Interdisc/1978/Produced in Argentina

Description: 7" LP. Theme/Muchacha Excepcional by Sandy Barber. Cover features artwork of a caped Lynda Carter as Wonder Woman.

Item: Theme from the ABC Series Wonder Woman LP "Mulher Maravilha"

Manufacturer/Year: Old World Records/1978/Produced in Brazil

Description: 7" LP. Theme Wonder Woman/The First Time by Sandy Barber. Cover features artwork inspired from Wonder Woman.

Item: Theme from the ABC Series Wonder Woman LP

Manufacturer/Year: CBS-Saban Records/1979/Produced in France

Description: 7" LP. Theme Femme Du Ciel (Wonder
   Woman)/Mightor by Michel Jourdan. The B-side
   features the theme song for Hanna-Barbera's
   "Mightor."

Item: Theme from the ABC Series Wonder Woman LP
Manufacturer/Year: Warner Bros. Records/1979/
   Produced in France
Description: 7" LP. Theme Wonder Woman/Superman
   (movie theme song) by Marylene/Laurent Bardy. One
   side of the cover features an image of Wonder
   Woman with hands-on-hips pose with Paradise
   Island in the background. The other side contains
   a picture of Superman.

Q CLOSE-UP

Lasso of Truth with Clark Brandon, Episodes #56 & 57: "The Boy Who Knew Her Secret Parts 1 & 2"

How was it working on the Wonder Woman *set?*

I was in my mid-twenties playing younger. My tongue was in my cheek through the whole thing. The show started on ABC and then went over to CBS. When I was on that show, I did a lot of work with CBS. That is how it even came about. They wanted to replace Lyle Waggoner. For me, a series is a nice world to be in. It was a big-time show—everyone had huge trailers and good food and it was an old-style CBS star show. She held that identity.

Lynda really ran the set and ran the show. She had her attention toward every detail. Her husband, Ron Samuels, was always there. It was really her show and her set. The one thing I remember, every day at a certain time, which was to the minute, she would wrap it. She would be in the middle of a scene and that would be her time to go. When she left, the whole crew was required to say, "Good night, Lynda." I remember that being a wonderful quirk about that set.

Where you a fan of the show?
I was a fan of Lynda; we did a lot of CBS stuff. I love one-camera, one-hour shows. I like the pace. I like the money. *Wonder Woman* was a fun opportunity. It would have been a lot of fun if we went into it the next season. They said we'll probably only do one season if we even do it.

So you asked to be a new character for the next season?
Yes. The episode was sort of a pilot. They were trying to do a pilot because Lyle wasn't going to come back. Then the show was canceled so nothing came of it. Lyle was gone and we were going to be the pilot.

You can see the genius of the network . . . to get a teen idol in there and that would bring a younger audience. I think that was the strategy. It would have been fun for me, but I don't think it was a youthful show; it was too corny.

That was a Warner Bothers show and I knew the whole crew from several shows that I had done so it was almost like home for me to go to this crew. I'm sorry it didn't go.

Did you do your own stunt while riding the out-of-control horse?
Yeah, that was fun too! I was the kind of guy to say, "Yeah, I'll do that." I rode horses my whole life.

I thought I was pretty cool riding that horse. I looked like a dink when I look back at it. I'm glad I didn't have to make money as a stuntman because I looked like a wet noodle riding a horse. That was an adventure.

The show was very comic bookish. As they were laying out the next season, there was always going to be a lot of stunts such as horse riding or bike riding to do. It would have been a lot of physical fun.

Skip finds out after his brain is erased who Wonder Woman really is. How do you think that would have played out in the next season?
I think it would have been the Jimmy Olson/Superman relationship. Wonder Woman and Skip would have always been obligated to be together because I did know her secret and I'd have to be sure the lasso would never go over my head again.

It would have been like, I'm just trying to be a superhero can you stop getting in my way. Then we would sneak in and before you know it she's not doing what she needs to do but rescuing me from making several bad moves. It would have been that relationship. It would have humanized her a little.

Bibliography

Davidson, Bill. "From the Pages of Comic Books . . . ," *TV Guide* 25:1244 January 29, 1977.

Mangels, Andy. "Backstage Pass Continued: Wonder Woman: TV Allies and Associates Dossier," *Back Issue* 1:5 (37–48) August 2004. (order at www.twomorrows.com/)

Maronie, Samuel J. "Wonder Woman: Out of Circulation but Destined for Syndication," *Starlog* 4:28 November 1979.

Morris, Brian K. "Backstage Pass: Lynda Carter: She's Still a Wonder" *Back Issue* 1:5 (17–35) August 2004. (order at www.twomorrows.com/)

O'Hallaren, Bill. "Her Golden Lasso Doesn't Capture Every Heart," *TV Guide* 29:1491 October 24, 1981.

The Internet Movie Database, www.imdb.com, Wonder Woman page.

Wikipedia.com, Wonder Woman page.

Wonder Woman: The Complete First Season, (DVD); Commentary from Lynda Carter and Douglas S. Cramer. Warner Home Video, June 2004.

Acknowledgments

The warmest Paradise Island kisses to Lynda Carter. For being the real Wonder Woman of our times.

A lasso of thanks to producer Douglas S. Cramer who was so open and giving to allow me to hear about the show from the man who made a true icon! Thank you so much. It meant the world to chat with you! You are a Wonder Man!

S. Sharp! What can I say: you were such a hoot to chat with! Thanks a million for taking the time to share your Wonder Woman office experience with me.

Leonard Goldberg! Thank you so much for taking the time to talk about your new feature film of Wonder Woman and allowing me to share with the fans your love and care with the film you are doing.

An ultraspecial thank-you to all the *Wonder Woman* guest stars who were so friendly and open to chatting with me about your experience on the series! A lasso of thanks to Stella Stevens, Joan Van Ark, Clark Brandon, Dick Van Patten, Vincent Van Patten, Bob Seagen, Kres Mersky, and Harvey Jason.

Andy Mangels, thank you for giving me great insight into the show you love so much! Thanks a million.

Glen Hanson . . . thanks again for another great cover and allowing me to share your wonderful art in the book! Thanks!

Thank you to all the celebrities, Perez Hilton, Jackie Beat, Glen Hanson, Julie Goldman, Gabriel Romero, Andy Mangles, Josh Zuckerman, Fernando Venutra, Allan Brocka, Peter Page, Chi Chi LaRue, Dylan Fox, Craig Taggart, Mark Padilla, and Fruit Salad's Rico & Pauly, who answered the Q&A's so truthfully without a lasso! Thanks!

A thank-you to the superfans of *Wonder Woman,* Mia Cruz, Vicki Mullins, and Kyall Coulton who took time to share their love of all things Wonder Woman/Lynda Carter with me!

Thank you to all the fine people—Dale Cunningham, Paul Florez, Anthony LaSasso, and Richard Fumosa—at Alyson Books who put in me faith to write a book outside my Angels expertise!

Peter Saenz and Toby Petty—thanks for your knowledge of *Wonder Woman.* I could not have done it without you both.

Charlene Tilton, you would have been a wonderful Wonder

Girl! But yes, you're right: the haystack fit you perfectly! You're such a Wonder Angel to me! xxoo

Many kisses and love to my mom and dad! Thanks again for being such special parents who support me in everything I do! I love you both.

Much love to my sister, Elizabeth and her husband, Rob and their two great kids, Jamison, and Kendrick. All four of you are simply the best!

To my friends who put up with me on a daily basis! Jules Massey, Julie Fick, Eric Thompson, Monica Holmes, Chris Kosloski, Shaun Neale, Ellen Loughin, David Chick, Morgan Slate, Josh Griffith, Sean Olson, and Dawn Robinson.

I have to thank Farrah Fawcett and Cheryl Ladd. for their support through the years. Who knew my favorite TV show would show me the path to writing books! (And I'm dyslexic!). I will always have angels looking over me!

Once again, a super wonder thank you to Scott Jonson, Brian Lamberson, and Joey Marshal, to whom this book is dedicated.

About the Author

Mike Pingel, writer, actor, and publicist, graduated from American University in Washington, D.C. He has written three books—*Angelic Heaven: The Fan's Guide to Charlie's Angels, The Q Guide to Charlie's Angels,* and *The Q Guide to Wonder Woman*—and is working on his fourth book, *The Q Guide to The Brady Bunch.*

Most recently Pingel made guest appearances in the Marc Anthony music video "Ahora Quien" and on Farrah Fawcett's reality series *Chasing Farrah.*

Pingel owns/operates several Web sites including www.CharliesAngels.com, and www.hollywoodFYI.com, and is the webmaster for www.CherylLadd.com and www.FarrahFawcett.us.

For up-to-date information on Pingel, please visit his Web site at www.MikePingel.com.